MULTICULTURAL MINISTRY

finding your church's unique rhythm

MULTICULTURAL MINISTRY

FOREWORD BY BILL HYBELS

DAVID A. ANDERSON

ZZONDERVAN™

GRAND RAPIDS, MICHIGAN 49530 USA

WILLOW
Willow Creek Resources

ZONDERVAN™

Multicultural Ministry
Copyright © 2004 by Willow Creek Association

Requests for information should be addressed to:
Zondervan, *Grand Rapids, Michigan 49530*

Library of Congress Cataloging-in-Publication Data

Anderson, David, 1966–
    Multicultural ministry : finding your church's unique rhythm / David A.
Anderson.—1st ed.
      p. cm.
    Includes bibliographical references and index.
    ISBN 0-310-25158-3
    1. Church work with minorities—United States.   2. Race relations—Reli-
gious aspects—Christianity.   I. Bridgeway Community Church (Columbia,
Md.)   II. Title.
    BV4468 .A53 2004
    253—dc22

2003023850

Interior design by Tracey Moran

Printed in the United States of America

04 05 06 07 08 /❖ DC/ 10 9 8 7 6 5 4 3 2 1

To the most awesome expression of heaven on earth—
Bridgeway Community Church,
you are way beyond my wildest dreams.
To my partners, core leaders, elders, deacons, staff, and volunteers.
Amber, Isaiah, Luke, and Asia—I love you.

CONTENTS

part 3

THE PRACTICAL GROOVE

part 4

THE LORD OF THE DANCE

FOREWORD

OFTEN I AM ASKED TO SPEAK AT WILLOW CREEK ASSO-
ciation churches for their anniversaries or capital campaigns. I
try to work as many of these as I can into my schedule, as I
never tire of seeing the work that God is doing in churches
today. God recharges my spirit and strengthens my commitment
every time I visit one of these churches.

David Anderson invited me to speak at the tenth anniversary for
Bridgeway Community Church. David had been an intern at Willow
Creek and had demonstrated his leadership gift and love for the
church during that time. Yet David's vision of the body of Christ was
different. His vision was of a multicultural church. He saw African-
Americans, Caucasians, Koreans, Latinos, and Jewish believers all celebrating the grace of God, who created beautiful and amazing
diversity within the human race. David saw not the suppression of
diversity but the blending of cultures in praise to God.

David faced many challenges to the vision. He had no models
from which to learn. He had no mentors to tell him how they had
beaten the challenges and achieved a similar vision. He had no books
that would give him guidance and wisdom from those who had
blazed the trail ahead of him. Many leaders in church planting said,
"It can't be done. One of the cultures ultimately will have to become
dominant and the others will die." In spite of what the experts told
him, David had one factor in his corner which gave him hope: the
vision he had was from God. God had planted it in David's heart and
kept it alive.

While God was building and growing a multicultural church in
Columbia, Maryland, he also started another work. This work was a

personal one in my own life, as God began to confront me with the sin of racism. I never considered myself a racist, yet I was ignorant of the effect of racism on our culture. One summer as I began to study the history of how our country had treated people from the African continent, God just turned me inside out. No words can describe the depths of anger, shame, and remorse that I felt. I was aware that God had started a work in my heart that would continue as long as I lived.

It was during this time of my personal growth in the area of race relations that I stepped into the banquet hall for Bridgeway Community Church's tenth anniversary. I had been following the growth of David's church for several years. In fact, David and Brent Zuercher had even come to Willow Creek to discuss their book, *Letters across the Divide*, as Willow Creek began a journey that would lead us to being committed to racial reconciliation. While I had been following the growth of Bridgeway, I had never been there, and I was not prepared for what God had in store for me that night.

I experienced one of the most unforgettable moments of my life that night. The splendor, joy, love, and redemptive potential of God's glorious church were shown to me in flesh and blood. The life change that I have seen in many Willow Creek Association churches was present at Bridgeway too—but it was different. What I saw that night were blacks, Latinos, whites, and Asians sharing how God had changed their lives, but God had also changed their view of the world to be more like his. They saw the value in others whose culture, skin, and traditions were different. They were not just tolerating one another; they were genuinely loving, laughing, and celebrating, as only those united by Christ can. That night I saw hope for the cure of racism, wherever it exists, through the work of Christ.

David Anderson writes on this subject of multicultural leadership not as an intellectual behind a desk but as a practitioner who at his core loves and believes in the body of Christ. David studies culture and current events on the topic of race. He has a weekly radio show that discusses how race is affecting America yet at the same time offers hope. He has talked with, listened to, and consulted with ambassadors and presidents in this country and from around the world. He has also developed the BridgeLeader Network to help organizations, churches, and institutions improve their multicultural effectiveness. David wants to take to the world God's vision of hope, which he saw come to life before his very eyes at Bridgeway.

If you believe there is no solution to the race problem, I ask you to learn from one who is on the front lines. Allow God to change the darkness and hopelessness of racism with a new vision of the church, because the church *truly* is the hope of the world.

—*Bill Hybels, Senior Pastor*
Willow Creek Community Church

INTRODUCTION
Can You Hear the Symphony?

WONJU PLAYED HER VIOLIN WITH DELICATE STROKES and fine discipline. The result was calming and captivating. Hearing her was an unforgettable treat as this petite Korean woman engaged her instrument with skill, focus, and pure beauty. When Wonju performed on the platform of Bridgeway Community Church one Sunday morning, what I noticed about her prelude was not only its simplicity and beauty. She was accompanied by a piano and a few other instruments. Now, Wonju plays violin for the Baltimore Symphony Orchestra. I am sure she could have played her violin solo. But the accompanying instrumentation lifted the entire sound to a melodious level of beauty that stirred the emotions of the assembled crowd.

As a professional, Wonju knows how to make her instrument sing with ninety-five other instruments under the leadership of a skilled conductor. How foolish would it sound if all the orchestra members played separately or off different pages of music for the duration of a concert. Although each instrument can be played alone, it takes the participating company of all instruments to truly make music.

All too many Christian churches in North America are simply one section of an orchestra. Some churches represent the string section. Others represent the percussion section, the brass, or woodwinds. For the sake of analogy, imagine these sections representing races and cultures that have distinct and separate qualities of sound. In and of themselves, these sections are unique and can stand alone. But when orchestral music is skillfully scored and executed, harmony fills the room and the soul. Such orchestral sound can take one's breath away.

Wonju invited my family to one of her symphonic performances. What a treat awaited me. When I experienced her performance with the Baltimore Symphony Orchestra, it was no longer about her single violin shining above a few other accompanying instruments. Now the focus was on the orchestra as a whole producing an unbelievably moving sound within which the violin was an integral part. Wow! This symphony was a higher level experience I had not known the last time I heard Wonju.

Haven't many of our uniquely skilled North American churches been sectioned off to such a degree that they have never known such an orchestral union? How foolish would it be for the American church to remain divided like that. The symphonic sound of a skillfully scored, well-executed concerto is a higher level experience than many churches have known.

This is why I'm passionate about writing this book! I'd like to paint a picture and give practical insights on how to bring the sections of God's orchestra together so that the world can hear a sound unlike they have ever heard before. The white church, black church, Asian church, Latino church—the whole church must come together under the skillful conducting of the Lord, Jesus Christ. The biblical score has been written and arranged. God is calling his players to perform their parts together in harmony with Spirit-empowered precision.

This is a new sound that the world is not used to hearing. The sound is not always classical. Sometimes it is rocky, funky, and yes, even groovy. But it is always full of soul (rather than solo!) as the diversity of God's instrumentation comes together on the stage of multicultural expression. As church members and visitors alike are being drawn in by the beauty of such music, everyone is beginning to feel the beat of the church's new groove. Are you ready for the music to begin? Can you hear the symphony? It can make a difference in your church!

part 1

THE SOCIAL
SWING

chapter one

THE BOOKENDS
Or "House on a Cul-de-sac"

THE HOUSE WAS LARGE, THE YARD WAS BIG, AND THE majestic pine trees that lined the back yard reached toward the sky with a sense of grandeur.

My father was so proud as he drove us through the beautiful suburban neighborhood in Adelphi, Maryland. We children sat in the back seat peering out the car windows, making sounds like *ooh* and *ah*. Dad explained that the neighborhood we were driving through was going to be ours. The split-level house on Rambler Place that he and Mom had purchased would be our new home. Feeling both pride and disbelief, my mouth open and my eyes as big as saucers, I nervously waited for the "just kidding" punch line. It was hard to imagine that we could live in such a nice home, in such a quiet neighborhood, on a street that ended in a word I had never heard of before—*cul-de-sac*. Like the Jeffersons in the barrier-breaking television show from the late 1970s, we were indeed "movin' on up to the east side." I was ten.

Shortly after the big move, we received a shocking "welcome." One morning I rolled out of bed, headed to the kitchen, looked out the window, and spotted police cars in our driveway. "What's the matter?" I hollered. My mother informed me that someone had placed a large cross in our front yard. She also said someone had driven a car across our lawn, leaving skid marks on our green grass and mowing over our delicate Dogwood tree.

I was confused. I could not understand why anyone would drive across our lawn. But the cross was a good thing, right? As the son of a Baptist preacher growing up in a good Christian family, I knew the cross represented hope and promise. However, while Dad was still out with the police, Mom explained to me that this cross was not a sign of hope but a symbol of terror. It was an act of hatred and a federal offense. We were unwanted in this neighborhood. I felt sad. I felt scared.

Within a couple of days, the phone rang very early in the morning. Because the phone was on my mother's side of the bed, she picked up the receiver only to hear a long period of silence before the caller hung up. There were other calls. One morning a muffled voice strongly suggested that we should move out of the neighborhood before it was too late. Later I asked if we were going to move. Mom stated in no uncertain terms that God blessed us with this home and *we were not moving.* Although I admired my parents' strength and courage, I cannot say that I was as certain as they were about sticking around. Someone was turning the neighborhood of our dreams into a nightmare. I felt mad. I felt nervous.

I believe it's correct to say that many whites in America were not raised to compensate for their whiteness as a liability. They may have been taught that they can grow up to be whatever they wanted to be. So was I. However, I had additional lessons to learn. My early experiences taught me at a young age that being black in America was a liability, not an asset. The determination of my parents to beat the odds was a value that I caught. I admired them then and still do to this day! One of my lessons was that though I could be anything I wanted to be, I would have to work harder and be smarter than my nonblack counterparts. I was taught that the resistance to my success as a minority in a majority culture was a reality that I would have to overcome.

THE PRINCIPLE OF BOOKENDS

Bill Brogan was a white boy who lived on the other side of the neighborhood. Billy and I became good friends as we rode bikes and played sports together. Our interracial friendship was never much of an issue. Billy did not seem to mind that I was black. I didn't mind his being white. We just treated each other like buddies. I appreciated our friendship.

It wasn't until junior high school that we separated along the lines of race. We didn't mean to, but it seemed natural. There were Asians and Latinos at our school, but they were few in number. There were more blacks and whites, and the racial divide between them was wide. Billy and I would see each other on the bus, but by then we were quite segregated. We lost touch. Worse, negative racial talk among the groups seemed to escalate. Blacks would talk about *honkies* or *crackers*, and whites would talk about *niggers* or *spooks*. I remember *chinks* and *spics* were terms used of Asians and Latinos.

I do not have many pleasant memories of junior high school. Blacks and whites were at opposite ends of the spectrum. I call them the bookends.

In the school library we were taught how books are categorized. In my office today I have a number of books on my shelves. Whether in the school library or in my church office, the principle of bookends holds true, namely, that at the beginning and end of each row of books are two books between which all the others lean. No book can stand alone. All of the books rely on each other in order to stand straight in a row. The books on the ends provide the necessary tension to keep upright the books in the middle.

Likewise, in North America tension exists between blacks and whites. I consider blacks and whites as the bookends of the racial debate in America. Consider the middle books as the other races and ethnic groups in North American culture. If the books on the ends move closer, all of the books will come together.

But the middle books also matter. Although Asians, Latinos, and other groups have their own set of ethnic issues, they have an important contribution to make, much like a middle child who is caught between battling siblings. Sometimes the best thing a middle child can do is to stay out of the fight. At other times the presence and peacemaking of the middle child can bring healing. Latinos are a large presence on the American bookshelf of knowledge. Koreans, Chinese, Native Americans, and Arabs, to name a few, also are a presence. All of the middle books can inform our great country on how to appreciate its multicultural richness.

I firmly believe that the entire shelf of books has knowledge and perspectives to offer the attentive reader. Exposure to the various books on the shelf, or cultures on the street, can add value to one's life experience. Such exposure can come by what I call proactive intent or reactive demand. For example, I have hundreds of books in my library, many of which I have never fully read. However, when a crisis arises, I scour my shelves to search for as much knowledge in that subject as I can. Demand makes me become quite intentional. But notice that the driving force is reactive and not proactive. As neighborhoods, corporate institutions, and churches begin to deal with the changing demographics of our culture, wise learners are beginning to proactively investigate the multicultural resources within their reach. But regardless of whether we go to our shelves motivated by crisis or by Christ, we'll find them overflowing with information and perspectives that can help us move the bookends toward each other for the glory of God.

If only more churches would reach out to the various cultures around them with the wonderful news of Christ. Christian community can be found with each book on the shelf. The problem, as I see it now, is that there is "white book Christianity" at one end and "black book Christianity" on the other. Then you have Latino Christianity, Korean Christianity, and even Jewish Christianity somewhere in the middle. Can you imagine if the books were bound into one massive almanac of rich knowledge and multicultural expression? Although there would still be many volumes throughout the world, they would continually point to the same author and finisher of our faith, the Lord Jesus.

What would it be like if churches around the world were known as places of such great love that the boundaries of culture, class, and color were shattered? A place where there were no bookends; just one big book of love with many chapters—one author with many stories. What a reference book this would be for a dying world. Moreover, what if we found that each of these books bound into the almanac were filled not simply with words but also with worship? What if we discovered that each book had a particular line of praise that when performed with the others became a symphonic chorus of masterful proportions? Only God could orchestrate such an arrangement. Could it be that he has? What would one title such an amazingly multicultural, multifaceted, multidimensional book of love? Perhaps—*The Church*!

AS IT IS IN HEAVEN

Have you heard of the term *timbre?* It is a musical term for the quality of tone distinctive of a particular instrument. Now imagine two different instruments playing the same notes. Although the sound of each instrument is unique, when played with the other instrument a new sound, a new timbre, is created. Different instruments, same notes; a uniquely beautiful sound.

Such a sound cannot be played without coordination. Have you ever heard an orchestra warming up its instruments? It's one of the worst sounds one can hear. But once the conductor steps up to coordinate the musicians, harmony fills the room.

The Lord Jesus is the conductor of our orchestra. He is also the author of each fragmented portion of this book called the church. He knows how much latent expression of worship the church has neglected to tap into because some have either refused or failed to learn from other cultures. In Jesus' prayer modeled for his disciples in Matthew 6, he said that we ought to pray "thy kingdom come, thy will be done on earth as it is in heaven." Could it be that we cannot understand what the kingdom of God on earth is supposed to look like because we don't have a clear view of what the kingdom of God in heaven looks like? I believe so.

Can you imagine segregated worship services in heaven? Are there only white Anglo-Saxon Protestants in heaven? Black Baptists? Korean Presbyterians? Latino Pentecostals? Of course not!

According to the apostle John, the writer of the book of the Revelation, a delegation of saints will worship the Lord in heaven: "And they sang a new song: 'You are worthy to take the scroll and to open its seals, because you were slain, and with your blood you purchased men for God from every tribe and language and people and nation. You have made them to be a kingdom and priests to serve our God, and they will reign on the earth'" (Rev. 5:9, 10).

Notice the people described in this heavenly scene. They come from every tribe, language, people, and nation. This vivid picture of the church purchased by the blood of the Lamb is not only in the mind of John but in the heart of God. Can you picture such a colorful rainbow of saints singing a chorus of worship and praise to the Lamb of God here on earth, as it is in heaven?

While I was completing some research at Oxford University recently, I decided to visit the historic and well-known All Souls Church in London. Sitting in the front row of the church, I could not help but glance back throughout the service. The beauty of this church was awesome; the preaching of its rector, the eminent pastor, writer, and apologist Dr. John Stott, was insightful; and the music was lovely. But it was the array of nationalities that amazed me. I was greeted by people from all over the world. They seemed to be from every tribe, language, people, and nation. How could one not think, *This must be what heaven is like?*

I'm sure that the apostle John did not simply gloss over his vision. He must have lingered. He must have been captivated when he found himself peering into a multicultural worship service in heaven. If you would allow me some creative license, I'm sure that if he were writing in today's language John would express his vision something like this: "Wow, I was amazed when I saw brothers and sisters from every conceivable people group worshiping our savior. They came from every nation and ethnic background. Some had slanted eyes and straight hair. Others had dark skin and thick lips. There were men and women, light and dark, young and old, worshiping our God with sincere hearts."

Should this not also be the picture of your church and mine here on earth, as it is in heaven? We have various tribes, languages, and people groups within reach. All those who have been purchased by the blood of Christ qualify to be in your church, do they not?

If this is true, then why don't they come? Why don't whites walk through the doors of many black churches? Why don't Hispanics worship with non-Hispanics? Why do blacks skip nonblack congregations? What keeps Koreans away from Caucasians? Why do blacks, whites, Asians, Indians, and Latinos all go to separate churches on Sunday mornings? Why is 11:00 A.M. on that day still the most segregated hour of the week?

Are the bookends so far apart that they cannot come together? Is there no real possibility for a multicultural almanac that provides a symphonic chorus of worship to the living God? I beg to differ. Even if you live in an area that is predominately one color or culture, people will travel to meet their needs. We are living in a time when very few churches are simply "community" churches that reflect only their immediate community. In many metropolitan, suburban, and even rural areas, churches have become quite regional. This means that people will drive past six or ten other churches just to get to the one that meets their needs, inspires their hearts, and informs their minds.

At our church I give thanks to God that I have heard an orchestral timbre. I have experienced harmony. I have absorbed the beautiful expressions of a multicultural symphonic chorus of praise. I have witnessed the church's new groove firsthand on Sunday mornings at Bridgeway Community Church in Columbia, Maryland. Multicultural ministry is possible, probable, and practical. When I visited All Souls in London, I was awestruck. Every week at Bridgeway Community Church, I am in a continual state of awe. The church is amazing! Not only do I get to look out at this multicultural congregation when I preach but we all get to do life together.

CONCLUSION

In the same way that my friend Billy and I were forced apart by the segregated world of our junior high school, our church environments have forced believers into earthly church patterns—as it is *not* in heaven. Heaven is not segregated. Heaven is not divided. Neither shall it be in our church. What about yours?

Although Billy and I have moved out of the neighborhood, his parents and my mother are still living there after all these years. And guess what? The neighborhood is completely integrated. There are blacks, whites, Asians, Latinos, and others. My mom has black neighbors living on one side and white neighbors on the other. Her neighbors across the street are Chinese, and two doors down there is a Hispanic family. Although it has been more than twenty years since I've lived there, every time I drive onto our street I am reminded of the price my parents paid. Not the financial costs but the emotional price of moving our family into uncharted territory, where we had to learn new ways of relating and enduring. But it was worth it. My family gained a much nicer home, and the neighborhood eventually gained the beauty of multicultural living. Through it all, I not only learned a new word, cul-de-sac, I learned about the rhythms of race.

The Christian church may have to relate differently and endure certain costs in order to achieve multicultural unity. But in the end, we will learn new words, new ways, and new worship. The beauty of our coming together will far outweigh the lesser beauty of our individual instruments and our segregated books. As the church of Jesus Christ resounds with its great symphony of praise on earth as it is in heaven, the world will see and hear a compelling sound of Christian unity. They will read the church as a relevant book of

God's love—a unified almanac with one unending story of God's grace and peace.

In the next chapter, we will learn that Bridgeway Community Church and All Souls Church are not the only ministries reflecting the multicultural kingdom of God. Others are stepping onto the dance floor of multicultural ministry.

chapter two

GET ON THE DANCE FLOOR

D O YOU REMEMBER THOSE SCHOOL DANCES BACK when you were in high school? Not everyone came but almost everyone wanted to. There was a lot of pressure at those dances. If you couldn't go with a date or a group of friends it was better not to go at all. Otherwise you might find yourself all alone with a plastic cup of watery red punch watching everyone else talk, laugh, and dance.

Then the deejay spun that one song you really liked. It had just the right melody and that familiar beat. Your desire to dance bubbled from the inside out. But wait, you couldn't dance alone. How geeky would that be? Worse yet, you didn't even know if you had the ability to dance. How embarrassing would it be to get on the dance floor with two left feet? You secretly hoped that a dance train would come by and sweep you away from that wall you'd been holding up. Or better yet, that someone of the opposite sex would actually walk over and invite you onto the dance floor with all of the other toe-twisting hip shakers.

Put yourself in that scene. You begin to muster up just enough courage to step out onto the edge of that floor. For the first time you realize there are others on the dance floor who are without partners. Their dancing doesn't look perfect. You're encouraged. You've gained enough strength to take that bold first step. You resolutely put down your red punch and begin to shimmy your way out onto the dance floor. As you shake your shoulders and wiggle your hips ever so slightly, your foot-tapping, head-bopping, finger-snapping body begins to feel a sense of rhythm. You're far from perfect, but the freedom you feel, although it's a bit nerve-racking, is exhilarating. It's freeing. It's groovy!

You know what? Ministry is a dance. An art form, if you will. It's not science. The powerful movement of the Holy Spirit provides a sense of inner music as we dance on the floor of multicultural ministry. When dancing in ministry with people from other cultural backgrounds, many of us feel like that lonesome young person watching from the sidelines. We stand against the wall and observe the other dancers. We feel the beat and yearn to get on the dance floor and shake a leg. But we cower.

After this book, though, you will cower no more. In fact, no more wallflowers allowed! Today, I have good news for you. You can dance! And you are not alone.

Look who's on the dance floor of ministry. It's not just whites and blacks anymore. The multicultural trends are compelling us all to "shake a leg" toward a more melodious ministry. Put down your punch and observe some of the other dancers who are stepping onto the dance floor of multicultural ministry.

In this chapter I'll introduce you to seven churches from various backgrounds, churches led by pastors who are Korean, African-American, El Salvadoran, Bahamian, and Caucasian. In addition, I'll introduce you to parachurch organizations that are practicing the dance of multicultural ministry.

CHURCHES
Ambassador Bible Church
www.ambassadorbiblechurch.org

Ray Chang was pastoring a second-generation Korean church in Vienna, Virginia, when he invited me to be the guest speaker one Sunday morning. Because it is difficult as a pastor to get away on Sundays, I made an agreement with Ray. I told him that I would preach at his church if he would speak at mine. My church hadn't received the Word of God through a Korean voice box before. Ray did a phenomenal job and they loved him. (I'm not sure if I did as well at Ray's church as he did at Bridgeway, but it sure was a joy preaching to his people.)

Something amazing took place on the Sunday Ray Chang preached at Bridgeway. God began to speak to Ray's heart about multicultural ministry. Ray confessed to me that he had never seen such a beautiful body of multicultural believers. To make a long story very short, Ray resigned his church and within six months planted a brand new multicultural church known as Ambassador Bible Church in another section of Virginia. Bridgeway mentored and commissioned Ambassador Bible Church and assisted in giving it birth and stability. Now after several years, the church is about 90 percent Asian. The real testimony is that that 90 percent is mostly mixed between Koreans and Chinese, which is culturally significant.

Ray has moved on from Ambassador, but his Caucasian Canadian associate, Scott Barfoot, has taken the reigns of leadership. Scott is married to a Chinese-American woman who has joined him in ministry and together they're doing a fine job guiding the feet of Ambassador Bible Church on the dance floor of multicultural ministry.

Antioch Bible Church

www.abchurch.org

Former professional football player Ken Hutcherson planted Antioch Bible Church in the Seattle area about seventeen years ago with just a few people in a Bible study. Now his racially diverse church consists of more than three thousand attenders and is doing effective ministry to its community and through its daughter ministries around the country.

Hutch, as he is affectionately called, has taken on the issue of transracial adoptions in his state. With a heart to free the system of discrimination against whites, who have to pay more to adopt a child, Antioch has instituted a program in which orphans can be adopted free of charge. Since the program began a couple of years ago, Antioch has placed more than sixty children in loving homes.

Hutch, an African-American married to a German woman, jokingly calls his children German chocolate kids. But because the church is serious about reconciliation, blacks, whites, Asians, Native Americans, and others have found a home at Antioch.

Bridgeway Community Church

www.bridgewaycommunitychurch.com
www.bridgewayonline.org

A little more than a decade ago, my wife and I parachuted with flares into Columbia, Maryland, to start a multicultural church that would be creative, inspiring, and biblically based. We knew it would be difficult, but we were committed to the vision. Columbia is a multicultural area and we were hoping that this would increase the odds for success. The interesting and sad thing about Columbia is that while it is a racially diverse community of ninety-five thousand, it can count on one hand the number of churches that have any significant racial integration. This fact served as a reminder to me that intentionality is absolutely critical.

There were many challenges along the way. Church planting has not been an easy route. However, hearing church consultants speak against multicultural ministry in the early 1990s actually inspired in me a greater desire to overcome the hurdles. For example, one consultant said, "David, I have never seen a racially mixed church grow without one culture having to die. If there are blacks and whites in the church, then one of the cultures died within the church."

This statement perturbed me. (That's the nicest word I can use here.) I went back to my small church of fifty people, composed mainly of whites and blacks at the time. After repeating the consultant's statement, I looked at my congregation, threw my hands in the air, and bellowed, "Why can't we both die? Let's all make a pact to die to ourselves in order to build a new culture, a Christian multicultural army of devoted followers of Christ!" The resolve, the commitment, and the inspiration from that Sunday still lives on in the heart of Bridgeway Community Church. Today Bridgeway is 55 to 60 percent African-American, 13 percent Asian, Latino or other ethnicities, and 27 to 30 percent Caucasian. We celebrate the beauty in the body of Christ within our local congregation and it's rich!

Mosaic

www.mosaic.org

Originally a predominantly white Southern Baptist church in Los Angeles, Mosaic became biracial when the pastor at the time, Tom Wolf, motivated his people to evangelize the community around them—which was Hispanic. The influx of Hispanics grew until whites became the minority group in the church. After Wolf resigned in 1992, Erwin McManus—a Latino who was born in El Salvador—became the lead pastor. McManus integrated the leadership of the church, harnessed several art forms to communicate to the current generation, and encouraged ministry to the nearby Asian-American community.

Since 1997 the church has grown from five hundred to about fifteen hundred attendees and is roughly 40 percent Asian-American, 30 percent Latino, and 30 percent Caucasian and other groups. Mosaic has a good reputation for reaching people where they are.

New Providence Community Church

www.npcconline.org

About twelve years ago, Clint Kemp started a multicultural church near the city of Nassau on New Providence, an island in the Bahamas, where blacks are the majority and whites the minority.

I visited New Providence during the early days of Clint's ministry, preaching on racism. We held a forum on the topic after the service. Many issues were brought to the surface. One tense moment I particularly remember. A vocal black lady stood up, turned to the white Bahamians in the crowd, and said, "Tell us what you heard about us black Bahamians in your homes when you were growing up." Pastor Clint, a white Bahamian, admitted, as he had done publicly on other occasions, that he had been taught that blacks were lower class and not to be trusted. He confessed that he had to deprogram his mind of the prejudice of his childhood.

New Providence's racially mixed congregation of five hundred is a testimony of racial harmony to a culture that hides its racism and classism behind its picture-perfect palm trees and sparkling water.

Redeemer Presbyterian Church

www.redeemer.com

While Tim Keller didn't start Redeemer to be explicitly multicultural, he did have a heart and vision to reach mid-city Manhattan in New York, which, by its nature, means multicultural. By elevating Asian musicians, Redeemer grew with a racial mix of primarily Caucasians and Asians, with smaller percentages of blacks and other groups. Keller is seeking to renew the city socially, spiritually, and culturally.

Redeemer has a heart for the city and has, as a result, planted many other churches throughout the burroughs of New York to reach out to several different groups of people of various economic and ethnic strata. With mentoring and money, Redeemer demonstrates a clear commitment to extending God's love beyond the walls of a unicultural church.

Willow Creek Community Church

www.willowcreek.org/extension.asp

Willow Creek is a very large, predominately Caucasian church in the suburbs of Chicago. The senior pastor is Bill Hybels. Bill phoned me after reading my book on race relations and invited my coauthor, Brent Zuercher, and me to be in the services the weekend after Easter 2001. As it turned out, our book had helped to trigger the shift in Bill's heart and has had a role in the multicultural development of Willow.

On this morning, Bill Hybels was admitting, before nearly seventeen thousand people represented in four weekend services, his own need to learn and grow in the area of race relations. A shift in Willow's tectonic plates was in motion. The era of apathy toward racism and justice was being shed and a new era of determination toward honoring God as a blended body was real.

Since then I have returned to Willow for staff training, meetings, and other speaking opportunities which have led me to believe that what took place in 2001 was not simply a one-time visitation of the topic. In fact, Brent Zuercher, who attends the church, is on a new multicultural advisory board for Willow. Changes are slowly being made.[1]

PARACHURCH ORGANIZATIONS

BridgeLeader Network

www.BridgeLeader.com

BridgeLeader is a not-for-profit consulting organization that Bridgeway established after the success of a book on racial issues I coauthored. After receiving numerous requests for help in the area of

---

[1]To purchase the video of the service we did titled Bridging the Racial Divide just call 800-570-9812.

cultural diversity and race relations, we put our eight years of experience into forming a resource for churches, colleges, universities, and
businesses. We now host annual conferences called the Multicultural
Leadership Summit; regional miniconferences around the country;
roundtable discussions on the topic of race relations; church planting
retreats for those who want to shepherd multicultural churches; and
on-site consultations.

CCCU

www.cccu.org

The Council for Christian Colleges and Universities is led by Dr.
Bob Andringa and is a coveted organization for many institutions of
higher learning to be members of. CCCU provides training, leadership development, educational programs, and networking for college
administrations and faculties from around the world. Racial harmony
is one of the initiatives that Andringa and his organization have
focused on for a few years. In an attempt to strengthen intercultural
competencies throughout Christian Colleges and Universities, CCCU
convened a forum of college presidents and campus leaders to discuss a strategic plan for developing competencies in all areas of campus and educational life at the university level. I am pleased with the
work that the network of colleges is embarking upon and am proud
to have had a small part in the consultation process.

Practical Bible College

www.practical.edu
800-331-4137

A school in Binghamton, New York, Practical Bible College, has
gotten off the wall and onto the dance floor of multicultural ministry.
The school is led by Dr. George Miller, for whom the issue of race reconciliation became personal a few years ago.

Miller recalls in his book, *Hope Grows in Winter* (Kregel, 2000), receiving heartbreaking news that his fifteen-year-old daughter was pregnant. I'm sure you can imagine how challenging this was to a godly father who also was a Christian leader in his community. Not only was Miller going to be a grandparent to his child's child, but his Caucasian family had to be prepared for something more. The father of the child was black.

The birth of grandson Keenan triggered in Miller a realization that his previous "neutral" stand on matters of race weren't acceptable to God. Miller explained to me that he had been neither active in nor resistant toward reconciliation initiatives, just neutral, which he now saw was like being lukewarm in God's sight. Jesus says he would spew lukewarm believers out of his mouth (Rev. 3:16).

Once the issues of race became personal, George threw himself into multicultural relationships and interests that have enabled his mind and heart to grow—and the college along with him. Practical Bible College is intentionally becoming more multicultural. As a result of the efforts of the administration, the minority enrollment has increased from 5 percent to 11 percent in the last two years. The staff has become diversified, and the BridgeLeader Network team of consultants has done workshops, seminars, and adjunct teaching at the school on multicultural effectiveness. Miller, as president, teaches a course on race, which speaks volumes about his commitment to reconciliation. Practical Bible College is on the dance floor of multicultural ministry.

Salem Broadcasting

www.WAVA.com
www.ReconciliationLive.com

In June of 2003, Salem Broadcasting Network through its Christian radio station WAVA (105.1 FM and 1230 AM) in Washington, D.C., embarked on a first-of-its-kind, weekly two-hour talk show on race relations. I am the host of the show, and my cohost, Tracey Tiernan, fields the calls and keeps the conversation moving. Topics range from interracial relationships and romance to raising interracial children. We've discussed multicultural adoption, multicultural ministry, affirmative action, and many other topics that have yet to find a safe environment for biblical dialogue. WAVA and Salem Broadcasting Network are on the dance floor of multicultural ministry. If you would like to hear the show live and are not in the Washington area, check out their web sites.

⑤

You can do multicultural ministry. You can build multicultural relationships. You can reflect the glory of God in your rainbow of relationships. It will take your being intentional and it will take commitment, but grooving in relationships and ministry with those who are different in color and culture will add richness to your life and perspective to your faith. In the next chapter I will talk about our commitment to grooving.

chapter three

MOVIN' OR GROOVIN'?

THE DANCE FLOOR IS FILLING UP WITH CHURCHES AND organizations that are either starting out as multicultural ministries or are transitioning in that direction. As the dance train comes through, don't be a wallflower. The face of American culture is changing; thus the face of Christianity will change also. Hopefully!

Few churches become incidentally or accidentally multicultural due to changing demographics in their community, and those that do aren't prepared to handle the multiple problems that confront them, many of which could be avoided. Intentionality is critical as it enables you to leverage a multicultural vision ahead of the curve and provide a greater sense of direction. Intentionality equips churches to jump ahead of the pack instead of jumping on the bandwagon a day late and a dollar short. Such intentionality is biblically mandated (more on that in part 4) and culturally smart.

In this chapter, I want to call your attention to the swing in America's demographics. Our world is becoming increasingly multicultural. As our nation swings toward a more ethnically diverse society, unicultural churches will face a major multicultural challenge. Church leaders will have to decide whether they will get into the dance of multicultural ministry or remain wallflowers holding up the traditions of racial separatism. Many unicultural churches will have to decide whether to move or groove. Some will move as far away from ethnic and economic diversity as they can, while others will groove to the new beat the Holy Spirit is drumming up.

THE MULTICULTURAL FACE OF AMERICA

Did you know that by 2050 almost 50 percent of the American population will probably be racial or ethnic minorities?[1] The 2000 United States census data showed that the population of the non-Hispanic white majority dropped from 76 percent in 1990 to 69 percent. Three out of ten people in America are minorities, while 6.8 million people identified themselves as multiracial on the 2000 census form.[2] The rate of Hispanic immigration in recent years has made that population the largest minority group, surpassing blacks. The number of Asians is expected to grow to 22 million by 2010, and the number of black immigrants from the Caribbean and Africa, now well over one million, will triple by 2010. At this rate, the United States will have no single majority racial or ethnic group by the middle of the twenty-first century. The multicultural face of America is ever changing and ever shining.

As I was walking through London a short time ago, I was struck by how racially diverse the city is. I rode the underground tube with Caucasians, Asians, Africans, Latinos, Indians, Lebanese, and more. If I had closed my eyes for a few seconds and opened them again, I would not have been able to determine whether I was in London or Manhattan. Although the two cities are an ocean apart, the demographics seem so very similar.

Our North American cities are replete with diversity. What's more, I've noticed great diversity in the suburbs and not just in the big cities. For example, I was in Orlando as a consultant on diversity for business leaders. Not far from where we were meeting was a Wal-Mart. Although the pockets of racial groups in the Orlando area didn't seem to intermix as much as I'd thought they would, the story was quite different at the Wal-Mart. When I walked through the

---

[1]Jordan T. Pine, "Accurate Census Count of Minorities," DiversityInc.com (14 February 2001).

[2]Marlene L. Rossman, *Multicultural Marketing* (New York: Amacom, 1994).

doors, I found myself in the melting pot of America right there in the store. It was unbelievable! I bumped into Koreans and Puerto Ricans; whites and blacks; the disabled, the young, and the aged. On the one hand, I was surprised at how segregated Orlando is. Yet on the other, the one place where people cross racial, economic, and age barriers is in the Wal-Mart. Hmm. While churches worship uniculturally, Wal-Mart spans color, class, and cultural lines because they meet the common needs of various groups. Maybe we should be praying, "As it is in Wal-Mart, so shall it be in our churches."

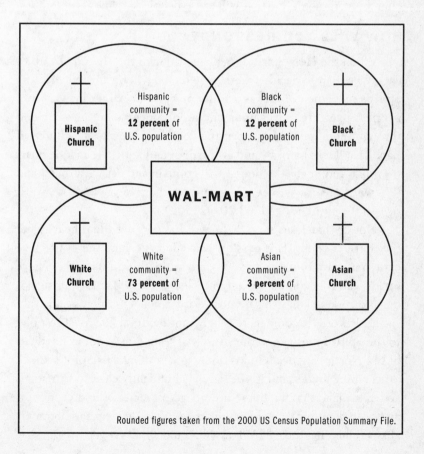

Hispanic Church

Hispanic community = **12 percent** of U.S. population

Black community = **12 percent** of U.S. population

Black Church

WAL-MART

White Church

White community = **73 percent** of U.S. population

Asian community = **3 percent** of U.S. population

Asian Church

Rounded figures taken from the 2000 US Census Population Summary File.

What's my point? If your vision for ministry doesn't include cultural diversity, your vision is not 20/20! It may be 1980s, 1990s, or even 2005, but it is not 2020. Maybe churches will learn how to be a place where everyone feels welcome, included, and valued. Maybe our churches will be places where the common needs of all people are met. When this happens, people will surface from pockets of obscurity. The common value that causes people to congregate in the Wal-Mart is the desire for a myriad of products for less money. Rich or poor, white or black, young or old, most people want to save money. What is the church's common value that will cause people to come together?

HOW WILL YOU RESPOND?

When the Holy Spirit does a new thing in the church, it's up to each Christian to decide whether he or she will be aligned with the Spirit's movement. God, as a gentleman, never barges his way into people's lives. He moves upon and around people but never in and through them unless they open the door. Jesus says to the church in Laodicea: "Here I am! I stand at the door and knock. If anyone hears my voice and opens the door, I will come in and eat with them, and they with me. . . . Whoever has ears, let them hear what the Spirit says to the churches" (Rev. 3:20, 22 TNIV).

Notice that Jesus says, "Whoever has ears, let them hear" what the Spirit is saying. Is it possible that God is calling the evangelical church in matters of race relations and multiethnic ministry? I believe so. His call is becoming louder and clearer every day as your neighbors, coworkers, children's friends, relatives, fellow students, and other social networks become increasingly multicultural. We must respond to the Spirit's message to the church of Jesus Christ not in Laodicea but in North America. God is doing a new thing. His Spirit's knock is becoming louder, and it's becoming abundantly clear to Christians across the land that the time for unity across racial, ethnic, economic, and even denominational lines is now. Church leaders and members alike are hearing the call. What will you do?

In our book, *Letters across the Divide: Two Friends Explore Racism, Friendship, and Faith,* my friend Brent Zuercher and I encouraged people to deal with issues of race on an individual level. From there, institutional change must follow. So I do hope your first response is a personal one. After that, maybe God will begin to burden all of our hearts for the reconciliation that will change the very face of our churches.

I am passionately convicted that the window of opportunity for racial and ethnic unity in the church is now open. On this issue, don't you agree that the church must be the head and not the tail? God has set the stage for our symphony to play at just the right time, hasn't he? If we as God's loving people continue to move away, gating up our homes and churches against the realities of a changing world, how can we reach that world? The music has begun, other dancers are on the floor, and the strobe light of God's Son is shining. Please don't leave the dance now. Open the door to your heart and to your church. Let's pick up our dancing shoes together. Shall we grab hold of our instruments and play the orchestral sound of unity? As brothers and sisters in Christ, let's purpose in our hearts to dance and make music together. Let's groove!

I appeal to you on behalf of Christ who moved into our world as a humble servant to reach us. He did not relocate heaven, moving away from the universe he created. He could have left us to ourselves and would have been justified in doing so. Yet Jesus humbled himself and became a bondservant in obedience to Father God (Phil. 2:6–9). Is this not the attitude we should have? Paul said that we are ambassadors of Christ as though God himself were making his appeal through us (2 Cor. 5:17–21). If we are called to be ambassadors of reconciliation, shouldn't reconciliation in Christ be the church's core value?

LET'S GET TO KNOW EACH OTHER

Even if we agree that reconciliation in Christ should be our core value, that doesn't mean that reconciliation, especially racial reconciliation, is going to be a cakewalk. If we are going to be ambassadors of reconciliation, we have to be honest with one another as multicultural brothers and sisters in Christ. Such honesty is not always easy.

We can tell house guests that they are welcome in our homes (and churches). We can tell them that our home is their home. But if we refuse them the right to touch the thermostat, hang their pictures, or place their food on the table for dinner, they will know the truth: they are not home, and it will be necessary to move. For people in our churches to feel at home enough to groove, we need a rhythm of cooperation, power sharing, and idea generation. If we refuse to allow diverse peoples to cooperate within the church, then we can't expect them to groove with us. The sharing of power, responsibility, investment, and accountability is critical for one to feel ownership, especially home ownership.

I've Got a Secret to Share

In the spirit of openness, allow me to share a secret. I have been part of several white churches. I cannot speak for all of my black brothers and sisters, and surely I will not try to speak for whites, Asians, Latinos, Indians, Arabs, Jews, Native Americans, or anyone else. But as an African-American I must confide in you something that makes me want to move and not groove, run and not settle, and sometimes even scream. One of my private struggles while I sat in some white churches or listened to conversations in white small groups or turned on white Christian radio programs was that I often felt like ultraconservative political ideas (not to be confused with conservative theology) were being strongly promoted. It wasn't promoted so much from the pulpit as it was coming from the ground level. The indiscriminate mixing of biblical theology with right-wing politics made it difficult for me to groove with you.

I wonder how many minorities in this kind of environment question how they can dance to an economic plan that's going to take welfare money out of their grandmother's purse. How can I groove to policies that equate personal responsibility with good Christianity while demonizing social action or affirmative action? We don't have to agree on politics. But we don't have to know each other's position on affirmative action to agree that there is a line that separates political ideas from true Christianity, do we?

I would often hear white Christian radio hosts and white evangelical publications emphatically state how badly our country needs to return to the values and morals of our Christian past. I'm just one black man, but I must inquire exactly what time in the past would that be for black people? To what time should we return? The time when my people were locked in the chains of slavery? The time when my people were under the oppression of segregation? Or the time of struggle for equality during the civil rights movement? I would rather look to the future. The future is what inspired my people to struggle forward, to press onward, to sing upward. The dream of a future day is what gave us extra strength to endure yesterday.

I just thought I would share this one secret because I really want to dance. I am not unaware that we are now living in a postmodern, post-Christian society. But please be aware that the coin of history almost always flips to tails for me as an African-American when I look back too long and too far. Understand that the music comes to a screeching halt whenever someone preaches politics in a way that adversely affects me or my people. It feels like my toes are being stepped on while we're trying to dance. If we are going to groove together on the dance floor of multicultural ministry, let's discuss our views on education, the economy, or the tax program as just that—views. To redefine political issues as "Christian" issues really makes true Christians who happen to be on the other side of the political spectrum question their commitment to Christ. Do you really want me to question my faith because you question my stance on non-moral issues such as bigger tax cuts? I hope not. Saddest of all is how many times I have been among white people (who assumed I was a

Republican) and heard with my own ears people question how any-one could be a Christian and be a Democrat. Likewise, I have been among black people (who assumed I was a Democrat) and heard the opposite charge. How this must grieve our Lord Jesus, who was, contrary to popular belief, neither a Democrat nor a Republican!

You've Got a Secret for Me Too!

Now, I have plenty of white friends who have told me how sick and tired they are of black preachers fanning the flames of bigotry from their pulpits. When I mention the polarization I feel as a black man in a conservative white church, my white friends quickly remind me how political and ethnocentric many traditional black churches are. I have to throw my hands up and agree. It's as if many black churches have been hijacked by the liberal wing of our political system. How can a white member feel at home in a church that continually preaches black empowerment and political favoritism? I learned that I am not the only one with a secret to share.

A Powerful Confession

Once a year, my consulting firm conducts a conference known as the Multicultural Leadership Summit. In this conference we usually like to bring together speakers who represent different platforms within the Christian community. A typical lineup of plenary speakers might include a Korean pastor, a white postmodern speaker, and a traditional black preacher. In one of our conferences, a well-known black preacher who was pastoring a large black church addressed the topic of racial reconciliation. After the preacher finished his fourth point on racial reconciliation, he paused and made a stunning confession. The preacher humbly admitted that for his entire ministry, he had been preaching afrocentrically. He confessed that the pain of his growing up black in the United States had tainted his preaching. He went on to say that as he preached through the book of Ephesians, the Holy Spirit began to convict him that he could no longer be afrocentric and Christ-centered at the same time. Although his home church had thousands of members, he stated that he wanted to grow his church to become more multicultural. After witnessing how multicultural the conference was, he admitted that though he had a long way to go, he wanted to make such strides.

This preacher's confession was so powerful that when he was done preaching, a white man in his fifties stood up and publicly apologized for the pain this preacher had endured. The preacher walked over to the tearful man and embraced him. As it was time for me to bring the session to an end, another man stood up—a young African-American male with a baseball cap turned backward on his head. He stated that he and many of his young friends had criminalized several Korean stores in the city, for which he was sorry. He asked the Koreans for forgiveness. Never have I seen the weeping of Asians in a public forum, but on this night, the tears were unstoppable. God was healing people as reconciliation was taking place right before our eyes. The power of truth in love was in clear view.

As I reflect on the preacher's statements, I can't imagine how difficult it would be for a group of nonblack attendees to feel at home in an afrocentric ministry such as the church this preacher was shepherding. I'm very happy this pastor desires to become less afrocentric and more Christ-centered. I pray that his vision was expanded by seeing what the kingdom of God on earth can look like.

Preaching Away White People

An African-American pastor in desperate need of help gave me a call. He said, "White people are coming to my church and I don't know what to do." This pastor was shepherding a church of about twenty-five black folk in a low-income, suburban community in Illinois. He could not explain why these white people were visiting. In fact, he confessed that whenever the whites would come, he would preach more afrocentrically and with more fire, hoping they would move on. Basically, he tried to preach them away. (This is definitely not a church-growth method I would recommend.)

The pastor didn't know that these white folks were visiting the church because they felt convicted by a Sunday service they attended at their large white church in the suburbs of Chicago, where my coauthor Brent and I were being interviewed. Evidently God stirred something up in this small group of white believers. In an effort to take action, they decided to visit this lower-income church. Can you imagine how they must have felt crossing these racial, cultural, and economic boundaries to attend this very small church? And then imagine a frightened African-American pastor wondering about the motives of these visitors—or "spies," in his mind. These good-hearted people were simply trying to build a bridge.

I asked the pastor if he could explain why he was so uncomfortable with the white attendees. He said he was fearful that these white folks were coming into his church to take over. In his mind, these educated doctors, dentists, and business people were going to give their money and then seek to control the church. He was afraid that they were going to, in his own words, "bring their white, conservative, right-wing evangelicalism" with them into his church and take over. By the time this pastor had called me, his church had grown from twenty-five to fifty; half black and half white. He had prayed for church growth for years, but this wasn't quite what the pastor had in mind! So now he was crying out for help. He needed to know how one grooves if one cannot move. How do you groove if those you want to leave will not move on?

Before I tell you what I said to this pastor, let's make some observations. Did you notice how the black pastor prejudged the motives of the whites based on his view of politics and evangelicalism? Did you notice how afrocentric he was in using his pulpit to preach empowerment? Black and white churches have traditionally been at opposite poles politically and culturally. Their ability to trust one another is very low. But no matter how suspicious the black pastor was, the visiting Christians refused to leave because they were on a reconciliation mission. They were at this black church to submit, to grow, and to learn, not to take over.

I suggested the pastor and his new white, female assistant pastor meet with me and a small group of his other white visitors to sort this all out. What a wonderful meeting this was for me. I had the benefit of watching reconciliation and true union take place. The joy of watching a black pastor submit to God's will for reconciliation was almost too much to bear. To see my white brothers and sisters submitting to the leadership of this pastor and, most of all, to the Holy Spirit was heartwarming. Instead of moving, they were committed to grooving. In fact, the large white church from which the visitors came allowed these outgoing members dual membership and partnered with the smaller church. Now this small biracial church provides free dental screenings and has a medical clinic to serve this underresourced community. Think about it, the community is being ministered to, the church is on a thrilling adventure, and most of all, God is glorified. There's nothing like the church's new groove!

One More Secret

The BridgeLeader Network brings together church leaders to discuss multicultural ministry in roundtable discussions across the country. During one of these discussions a short while ago, a Korean church planter raised his hand and said, "I'm tired of the racial reconciliation discussions being between blacks and whites. Koreans and others are a part of this country and the Christian church too. I think they ought to be in more leadership positions in your church." I immediately agreed with the Korean brother and told him about my bookends illustration. I explained to him that, in the United States, whites and blacks are the bookends and that all the other cultures are in the middle. If the bookends come together, everyone else will get closer. The middle books, as I call them, have a lot of information that can help us all get along. He agreed. Then I looked over to one of my Korean deacons and said, "Will you, my dear middle-book brother, please close our roundtable in prayer?" Everyone laughed and we were joined in prayer. But the Korean pastor was right. He clearly communicated his secret: churches will not have a multicultural groove if reconciliation remains a biracial issue.

⑤

The world around us is changing demographically. The swing toward multiculturalism should encourage all of us to consider grooving with each other instead of moving away from the people God is bringing us. We shouldn't preach them away, and we shouldn't keep our secrets to ourselves as we silently slip out the back door. So how does one learn the dance of multicultural ministry? The next section of the book is devoted to teaching you some steps for grooving to the rhythms of racial and ethnic unity. Allow me the privilege of being your dance instructor.

part 2

THE RELATIONAL ROCK

chapter four

IS YOUR DANCE FLOOR SAFE?

M Y WIFE AMBER AND I TRAVELED TO ZERMATT, Switzerland, with another couple to enjoy a few days of vacation without the children. What an infusion of romance! Amber and I hiked around the foot of the Matterhorn mountain through knee-high snow. We held hands, walked through little shops, and ate at quaint restaurants. Most surprisingly to us, we danced in a hotel bar to live music. My wife is an introvert. Drawing attention to herself in the middle of a bar is completely outside her comfort zone. She also doesn't consider herself a good dancer. But with a little encouragement from our friends, and the bartender, the four of us hit the floor and did our thing. True, Amber wouldn't make Jennifer Lopez jealous, but she did loosen up. We laughed a lot as we stepped on each other's toes. Boy, what fun!

Relationships are like dancing. Relating to other people often brings together opposites who complement one another.

There are different styles of dancing too. The waltz, for instance, is a one-on-one, face-to-face, hand-to-hand dance that requires personal contact and closeness. Each move requires the opposite action by the waltzing partner.

Some dance steps are less personal. Take a line dance like the electric slide. Some relationships are more like this style of dancing, where dancers can be strangers and no personal contact is necessary. Everyone can learn the steps. Only music is needed. Before you know it, twenty-five strangers are boogying together.

In between is freestyle dancing. The interactions are not as intimate as waltzing yet not as distant as a line dance. A couple on the dance floor who begins dancing spontaneously as they create their own moves along the way is an example of freestyle interpersonal relating.

When it comes to race relations in North America, how do we dance together?

I have found that most of the time we do the electric slide. Whites, blacks, Asians, Arabs, Hispanics, and others tend to line-dance with one another in common areas, such as work projects, back-to-school night, or the weekly soccer game. The surface image is commonality and community. But when people leave the soccer field or drive home from work, it is as if the music has slowed down and the floor has thinned out. Unfortunately, for many of our interracial acquaintanceships, freestyling or waltzing is too threatening. In the electric slide the dancers don't have to know one another. Interracial relationships require give and take, leadership and followership, talking and listening, conflict and resolution. At times there may be the discomfort of stepping on each other's toes.

INTERRACIAL FRIENDSHIPS ON THE DANCE FLOOR

Your church, and mine, can and should provide a safe place where people can electric slide, freestyle, or waltz. Having a place where surface levels of relating are permitted is important. But progress is also important, and creating ministry opportunities in which people can serve together helps this progress tremendously.

Over the years friendships with some of my associates who are of a different race have developed because we were serving together. There are some men and women I have grown to love with whom I might never have developed a close relationship without that common ministry.

For example, Rich Becker was a friend from a singles group I pastored while interning at a large suburban church in Chicago. As far as I can surmise Rich would never have chosen me as someone to hang out with, and the feeling was mutual. Not that we were ene-mies. We just had nothing in common, or so we thought.

When it came time for me to leave my internship to plant a church in Maryland, I invited Rich to move with me. Because he ran sound boards and did video productions for the singles group, I knew his skills were in the areas where I was deficient. My vision for the kind of ministry I wanted to start captivated Rich. Not the multicul-tural part; as a Caucasian kid growing up in the white suburbs of Chicago, Rich hadn't developed much of a desire for racial reconcil-iation. It was his desire to reach unchurched people through the cre-ative arts that inspired his commitment. As I preached to the churched and unchurched alike, Rich complemented the message through the oversight and performance of music, drama, and multi-media.

During my internship Rich and I did the electric slide. But after he moved to Maryland with me to start Bridgeway Community Church, we advanced to freestyling in ministry. Rich's growth wasn't limited to his relationship with me either.

What transpired over time in Rich's heart was amazing to watch. Along with his passion for creativity grew a desire to learn how to reach all people. A subtle shift occurred from being seeker-targeted to all-people-targeted. It was as if a racial reconciliation conversion had taken place. Rich began writing dramas and crafting videos with racial insights that could have come only from a man who had been relating regularly with people of color beyond the electric-slide level. His leadership in developing a multicultural stage every Sunday was evidence of his passion for multicultural ministry.

Superb performance by spiritually and technically qualified ser-vants may have been Rich's previous definition of excellence. But his passion for multicultural ministry had expanded this definition. I'm sure that Rich, as the executive director of creative arts at Bridgeway, would now say that the Sunday service falls short of excellence if it is not executed by a multicultural array of quality servants.

What happened to Rich? I'm convinced that it was his freestyling with people of color. It is hard for people to remain unaffected when relating across racial lines on a regular basis. When you do life and ministry with people from various racial backgrounds, your thoughts, opinions, and ideas are bound to shift.

That is what happened to a black man name Joe Allen. When Joe first started to attend Bridgeway, he confided that he and his wife seldom, if ever, invited white people into their home. And, he inquired, why should they? "I have to work with them, live in the same neighborhood with them, and now at Bridgeway, go to church with them." Basically Joe was saying that when it came to relating to white folks, the electric slide was fine with him. Joe was content to have a private place where he could speak his language and play his music without worrying about how he was being perceived.

But as Joe grew in his devotion to the Lord and the church, he began to serve with Rich in the creative arts ministry. Relating to Rich and others in ministry became unavoidable. Because Bridgeway doesn't own a church building, the majority of church meetings and Bible studies take place in private homes. Through doing life in the creative arts ministry, rehearsals, video shoots, and meetings at his home, the time came when he was challenged to move to a more personal form of dancing with whites in our church. The music was slowing down and he developed closer forms of interpersonal contact. Joe was becoming a fully devoted racial reconciler.

What happened? I believe another racial reconciliation conversion took place. Such a conversion occurs when people realize that there is a racial problem in North America, in the church, and even more specifically, in their lives. These budding converts conclude that when it comes to race relations, they are either a part of the problem or a part of the solution. They realize, like Rich, that being unaware or uninvolved is not a part of the solution but a part of the problem. They realize that, like Joe, locking others out of their private world to protect their privacy doesn't help solve the problem of race.

Bridgeway provided a place where both of these men could coexist in ministry. It provided them a dance floor where they could move from the electric slide to the freestyle of serving together. Rich and Joe are a terrific tag team within our creative arts ministry, and their relational waltz has served the kingdom of God immeasurably. Rich's family and my family have been waltzing for more than a decade now. Our families have done life together as we've progressed from singleness to marriage to parenthood. Rich and I hang out almost daily as we discuss life and ministry. It is hard to imagine ministry without him. We are a terrific tag team as well.

I long to hear countless stories of brothers and sisters in the body of Christ—blacks and whites, Koreans and Chinese, Puerto Ricans and Mexicans—waltzing together in ministry. What a joy ride it can be. For us, it has been fun and fulfilling.

SLOW DOWN BEFORE YOU SLOW DANCE

However, let me caution you. Moving too fast from the electric slide to the waltz may be much too threatening for some. Changing the music in one's ministry too quickly from an upbeat tune to a ballad tends to clear out a dance floor in record time. It would be wise to transition the music from a fast tune to a medium-tempoed song to help those on the dance floor adjust. As people begin to freestyle at their own pace, they will find their own rhythm of relating. From the medium-tempoed freestyle, people will begin to find others with whom they can slow dance or waltz.

For example, if Bridgeway did not provide service opportunities where people like Joe and Rich could relate, then they may have never learned how to relate in ministry as real brothers in Christ. And if there were not a multicultural church where they both could coexist, I doubt they would have ever been on the same dance floor of ministry. At Bridgeway we provide people with the opportunity to progress at their own pace. The operative word is opportunity. If people want to grow in their interracial relationships, there are many opportunities at our church to do so, from serving alongside people of different racial backgrounds to attending racial reconciliation seminars to participating in smaller focus groups on the topic. We encourage progression.

Once a church, a company, or a neighborhood provides the dance floor to do the electric slide, it would be wise to progress at a pace that is sustainable and respectful of privacy. For example, I encourage you not to walk up to a Korean person in your neighborhood and say, "Hi, my name is Jen, and I really want to develop an interracial friendship with you because I've been reading a book on race relations. Do you think we can get together every week over a bowl of kimchee and rice to talk about our cultural differences?" Although your neighbor may smile and nod, don't take that as a strong vote of affirmation. As your neighbor returns home, she may very well be wondering what you were smoking.

Consider a different approach. For instance, say you are working around the yard and see a few of your neighbors talking, one of whom is Korean. Maybe you should walk over to the group and introduce yourself. Make sure you memorize the Korean neighbor's name. After a bit of small talk about your lawns, your home, and your neighborhood, and so on, tell the neighbor, by name, how nice it was to meet her. Over time and after more small talk, as you pray and identify more opportunities for relating, other conversations may allow the acquaintanceship between you and your Korean neighbor to develop on an individual level. Now that you are communicating one on one and learning more about your Korean neighbor, you are becoming more comfortable with each other.

As the acquaintanceship develops, ask your Korean neighbor where she shops for food, goes to church, or works. You are now beginning to freestyle. Be willing to listen and learn and to explore new thoughts about family dynamics, as well as new tastes and smells. If you hear your neighbor speaking a different language with others, inquire how to say "hello" in their language. Restate it. Memorize it. As you are invited into the home of your Korean neighbor, or vice versa, realize that your relationship is growing and that trust is being developed. Over time, differences in background, religion, race, politics, child rearing, beliefs, education, and other values may surface. This will give you both opportunities to express your opinions. You may have the chance to invite your new friend to church. Continue to pray that God gives you the grace to be a vibrant and loving witness to this family, if they are not believers. If they are believers, you will be blessed to have discovered new fellowship with your Korean brothers and sisters in Christ.

THE SAFETY RULE

I met a white businessman, Brent Zuercher, in the same singles program in which Rich and I met. He was part of a men's discipleship group I had started. Brent and I could not have been more different. I am an extroverted African-American preacher who is visionary, big-picture oriented, and gregarious. Brent, on the other hand, is an accountant. Need I say more? (Just kidding!) Brent's detail-oriented mind allows him to think and process at impressive levels. As an introvert, Brent prefers small-group interactions, personal accountability, stability, and consistency. The singles group of one hundred and fifty was the dance floor for our electric slide, if you will. In the smaller discipleship group, we learned to freestyle.

But it wasn't until I moved into Brent's three-bedroom apartment that we went to deeper levels. As roommates, we found that we had a lot in common and nothing in common at the same time. We had singleness, a desire for pizza, a love of sports, and a serious walk with Christ in common. Yet our music, clothes, and other interests were different.

We really started to dance when I invited Brent to move from Illinois to Maryland with me to start a multicultural church. Brent confessed that one of the barriers that kept him from considering such a move was the fact that the church would be multiracial and that he had some issues with race.

I told Brent that it would be okay to write me a letter with his concerns, and boy, did he ever! Penetratingly honest questions like, Why are blacks so angry? Why is everything a racial issue with blacks? Why do I have to call you African-American? And who should apologize? They were followed up with pages of explanation and detailed thought. I responded with equal intensity by letter for three years.

The letters were published in a book titled *Letters across the Divide: Two Friends Explore Racism, Friendship, and Faith*. These letters were the interracial waltz between a black preacher and a white accountant. The music slowed, the conversation intensified, and we stepped on each other's toes from time to time. Because of the safety we found on the dance floor of our relationship, we were able to speak truthfully in love. Had I not been hired by that suburban church, which was 98 percent white, Brent would not have been exposed to this black preacher. Exposure opens up experience. Our common ground of singles ministry and discipleship provided us a dance floor where we could relate. Once we were in the same ministry, we were able to intentionally relate. People don't waltz by accident. Like Brent and I made a conscious decision to dialogue at deeper levels about race, conscious acts toward others who are different is a necessary step in building interracial friendships.

At the beginning of our letter writing, Brent and I made a commitment to one another that we would enter the process with honesty. We agreed that we would be open enough to say whatever we felt as long as there was respect. Brent had a no-holds-barred freedom to speak. He needed to know that he could stumble and bumble on the dance floor without being called a racist. Safety was critical. If there was no safety, then there could not be honesty. If we were not completely honest, then we knew the time we invested would be futile. Permission to speak freely was our one rule.

AM I A SAFE PERSON?

Brent and I have received many compliments on our letters' honesty, openness, and insights. But the most consistent compliment I have received on the book is that I was a safe person to talk to. The fact that Brent could ask such penetrating questions was proof to some readers that I must have been safe enough for Brent to feel this freedom. This observation eluded me until it was continually expressed. It prompted me to begin thinking about what it is to be a safe person who builds bridges of reconciliation.

Listening Ears

The first quality a safe person (and ministry) must possess is listening ears. The one advantage of communicating through letters with Brent was that I had time to read and reread his letters before responding. I also had time to write and rewrite. There were times when Brent stated things that made me drop the letter in disbelief. My disbelief would at times turn into anger. I would then fire back a retorting letter that would sit on my desk for twenty-four hours. Countless times I would reread the letter afresh the next day and be grateful that I had not mailed it yet. When you are conversing with someone face to face, even though you don't have the luxury of time to reflect on a written letter like I did, you can still listen nondefensively. Restating what the other person has said is critical to insure understanding, especially in heated debate. Patiently allowing people to finish their thoughts as you try to understand what they are saying and what they are meaning is critical.

Outside of debate, listening to another person's race story is powerful. Everybody has one. Just ask someone of another race what it was like growing up in this country as an Anglo, African-American, Asian, or Latino. After that, just listen. I have heard white friends say, "I've never thought of my race story. I don't think I have one." But then as the wheels begin turning in their mind, they begin thinking about how their upbringing and family frame-works have shaped their opinions and definitions about race. I didn't realize how sick and tired, and even frustrated, many whites feel regarding the topic of race until I listened to Brent articulate his feelings.

When I began entering Asian circles, I was surprised to overhear some of them speak of whites in some of the same ways I have heard within African-American circles. I used to think that only African-Americans had issues with how to relate, fit in, and navigate success when working within the majority culture. We all have a story. When someone asks a black man or woman what it was like to grow up black in North America, be ready to listen. I have found that listen-ing to someone else's story provides understanding and helps us to identify with one another.

Limiting Loaded Words

The second quality of a safe person is the ability to limit the use of loaded words. There is nothing more incendiary than using terms loaded with venom and emotional baggage. Using terms like "those people" will shoot you in the foot every time. Or worse, I have learned that the term *racism* or *racist* should be used only in extreme cases. If I, as a black man, describe as racist a statement that may really just be an ignorant comment, I will alienate the very person I'm trying to educate. I have learned to be more precise in my terminology, and I try to educate others by turning ignorant statements into teaching moments.

For example, I will never forget the time I was in the student din-ing room in Bible college. The room held about five hundred people. About ten of the African-American students were sitting together for a meal. I was sitting at a table with some friends, who happened to be all white. Then someone at my table said, "David, you're always preaching in chapel about unity and integration. The blacks are the ones segregating themselves." Referring to the table with the small group of blacks, he said, "Look at them over there." Although my brown skin didn't reveal how red my face felt, I was flooded with emotions.

After I took a deep breath, God graciously helped me to turn this statement into a teaching moment. I answered with a question. "Bob [not his real name], how many people do you think this dining room seats?"

He responded, "About five hundred."

"How many blacks do you see sitting together at that table?" I asked.

"About ten," he answered.

I then asked, "How many white people do you think are in this dining room, Bob?"

He approximated about four hundred and seventy.

Given the fact that four hundred and seventy of the people in the dining room were white and ten of the blacks were sitting together, I asked Bob to repeat who it was he thought was segregating themselves. He was dumbfounded when he realized that only one other table had black people at it while more than forty tables had white people at them.

One final question would drive the point home. I asked Bob, "Do you really think that it is fair to expect the ten black people to have the sole responsibility of integrating themselves into the four hundred and seventy of you at dinner tonight?"

"Of course not," he replied.

For the first time, Bob was able to see race from a different perspective. Had I answered his loaded question in the flesh instead of in the spirit of reconciliation, a fire could have started.

Loving Arms

A third quality of safe people is loving arms. While teaching a cultural diversity class for professionals at the University of Phoenix, I ended one of the sessions by asking the class to read one of the letters that Brent and I had written. Since the book of letters was still in manuscript form, I thought this multicultural class would be a good guinea pig.

A white woman volunteered to read Brent's letter to me, and a black woman volunteered to read my response to Brent. Brent's letter was on the question of why everything is a racial issue with blacks. It ended with Brent's final and emotionally charged statement: "Crying 'racism' every time an injustice is experienced or on every occasion that is not perceived as being completely positive for blacks as a whole does not elicit compassion nor does it motivate heart change in whites. I do not know how others feel but I am tired of the complaining, the excuses, and the finger-pointing."[1] After the woman finished the letter, you could have heard a pin drop.

Before allowing the next volunteer to read, I decided we needed to pause for breathing room. I asked the class what they were feeling. The woman who read the letter was visibly shaken and her face was flushed. Then tears began to stream down her cheeks. I gently asked her why she was crying. "This," she said, pointing to Brent's letter, "is the way I feel." She had never had a safe environment in which to voice such a concern. Brent's articulation was also giving credibility to what she had been feeling for a long time.

What happened next took us all by surprise. Before she read my response to the class, the black woman who had volunteered to read stood up and walked over to the white lady. She sat next to her, opened her arms of love, and surrounded the white lady in a comforting embrace as she wept. What a sight to see! I was amazed. This wasn't even church! These two strangers, one black and one white, were hugging because a safe environment in which real communication could take place elevated the class from mere instruction to

---

[1]David Anderson and Brent Zuercher, *Letters across the Divide* (Grand Rapids: Baker, 2001), 50.

healing. Loving arms communicate things that words are powerless to say.

⟨෨⟩

How unfortunate, but true, that even when we work on limiting loaded words and we try desperately to lend listening ears and extend loving arms, we will still experience frustration when dealing with race. As you turn the page to the next chapter, we'll explore together this frustration factor.

chapter five

THE FRUSTRATION FACTOR

ONE YEAR FOR OUR ANNUAL CHRISTMAS PARTY I treated my staff to a dinner boat cruise. As we sailed along the Baltimore Harbor, the deejay pumped up the jams. After dinner the dance crowd began doing a line dance most people knew. You guessed it, the electric slide. Many of my teammates and their spouses jumped up to boogie. Now, this black man can dance. I really do have rhythm. There is just one disclaimer. I have to freestyle and make the dance up as I go along. Whenever I need to learn a line dance, all the rhythm in my body goes on strike. You can imagine how frustrated I was when the music didn't match my freestyling version of the electric slide. For that matter, no one else's dance steps matched mine either. The crowd moved in one direction, and then another. But whenever I spun and turned, they went forward. Whenever I went forward, they were turning and spinning. They were all wrong! I was frustrated at their inability to move with my groove.

As you've wisely discerned, I was the one out of rhythm. Everyone else knew the moves and fell into step. As long as I was on the sidelines, it was fun to watch. But whenever I tried to jump in, it was frustrating.

I wonder how many of us feel this way when relating across racial lines. From the sidelines we admire the sight of racial unity, but we stumble when we can't get our groove to work. So we observe, but we fail when we try to participate.

Granted, race relations can be quite confusing at times. We're not sure whether to say black or African-American, Hispanic or Latino, Oriental or Asian, Anglo or white. We wonder if it is okay to ask someone whether they are Chinese or Japanese because, truthfully, some of us cannot tell the difference. Moreover, stepping out to start conversations is much like stepping out on the dance floor when everyone else seems to know the moves but we don't. For instance, when we are curious about someone's ethnicity, we're not sure how to inquire in a nonoffensive way. If we ask, "Where are you from?" they may say, "Illinois." Then we stumble, regroup, and say, "Ah yes, Illinois." Now we feel dumb and the other person may feel offended. (We should have simply asked, "What is your nationality or ethnic background?") You may think to yourself, *If only someone would take me by the hand and show me the dance steps, it would be so much easier*.

My wife, Amber, is Amerasian, which means she is part American and part Asian. Her biological father was an American soldier, and her mother was full-blooded Korean. She grew up in Korea. She spent many years in the United States feeling as if she fit in nowhere. Most Koreans would never guess Amber is Korean because her almond-shaped eyes are not slanted enough. Most Anglos or African-Americans on the other hand wouldn't see her as "American" because her eyes have just enough slant to them to make her look Asian. Because of her cinnamon-colored skin and dark hair, she has been mistaken for Hawaiian, Latina, Filipino, and a host of other nationalities.

When Amber first came to the United States she used to become very frustrated when people asked her, "What are you?" For a while her curt response was, "Human." Over the years, Amber learned that her response wasn't helping the reconciliation process. She has purposed in her heart to assist people by turning their question into a teaching moment. Now she helps the inquirer by clarifying the question. When asked, "What are you?" Amber now says, "Do you mean what nationality am I?" She then tells them her background. Amber would technically be correct if she said that she is American, since she is a U.S. citizen. However, because she wants to be a reconciler, she answers the intent of the question.

When I was trying to do the electric slide, another dancer came alongside me, took my hand, and assisted me out of my old rhythm into a new way of dancing. As my helper locked arms with me on the dance floor, we turned and spun together. Slowly, I began to pick up the dance moves. In a similar manner, Amber can be likened to a dance assistant as she helps others with how they inquire about ethnicity. Turning tactless questions or ignorant comments into teachable moments is a gentle way to guide someone who is stumbling onto the dance floor of race relations. If you and I are to become fully devoted reconcilers, it is our calling to extend our helping hand to those who want to learn how to relate across racial lines. Frustrated or not, we are not allowed to reject them out of exasperation if we are to be good ambassadors of reconciliation.

UNDERSTANDING THE FRUSTRATION

I have spoken with many white people who have made gallant efforts to reach across racial lines and have had their hands slapped in the process. White pastors will tell me how they have tried to reach out to black pastors only to be met with cold resistance.

I know of one white pastor of a very large suburban church in Texas who called a black pastor in the city, whose church was equally large. The white pastor extended his friendship to the black pastor and suggested that they get their churches together for fellowship and reconciliation. The black pastor rejected the white pastor's offer as insincere. "If you're for real," said the black pastor, "then have some of your white bankers extend loans to my black businessmen." The white pastor was somewhat offended by what he perceived was a put-off.

Nevertheless, a short time later the white pastor called again with some names and phone numbers. The black pastor passed on the information. Within one phone call, the black businessmen received loans. The black pastor called the white pastor back and said, "Let's fellowship. I now know that you are serious about reconciliation."

Here we had two frustrated pastors. The white pastor was frustrated by the black pastor's lack of open-armed warmth in receiving his invitation to walk together in ministry. The black pastor was frustrated by the invitation to walk together in ministry without proof that this was not another patronizing effort of a white Christian leader to appease his or her racial guilt. How can anyone dance under these conditions?

Allow me to use an analogy to explain the frustration of the black pastor. As a church leader who has done a fair amount of marital counseling, I am never surprised to see a recurring scenario among couples. Imagine a man calling to set up a counseling appointment for his wife and him. Picture their body language as they sit on the couch in my office. The wife's arms are crossed; she looks emotionally shut down. The distance between the two of them is as much emotional as it is physical. After a little preliminary chat, I ask the couple how long they've been married. "Thirteen years," says the husband. Then I ask, "What has she been trying to tell you for the last thirteen years that you are just now hearing?" The woman looks at me, wondering how I knew. For the first time in a very long time she starts to feel as if someone might understand.

I have found that most men don't call for counseling until it's virtually too late. This wife has been complaining for years and years, and yet the husband has been oblivious to the seriousness of his wife's concerns. The anger and lack of validation have finally caused the woman to shut down emotionally. After suggesting the idea of counseling for years, she is done dealing with this same issue over and over again. She is ready to move on. It is then that an alarm goes off in the mind of the husband and he finally senses the seriousness of his wife's resolve. He thinks, *Yikes! We have problems. I'd better call a counselor.*

Put yourself in the counselor's shoes. What would you say to this angry, frustrated, and wounded woman who has been crying for change for thirteen years, to no avail? What are you going to ask of her? Maybe you would ask her to explain her viewpoint on the relationship. Maybe you would ask her where it all began. Maybe you would suggest that she give her husband one more chance. But she's done all that already, many times. How can she be convinced that this insensitive, unchanging husband has had a conversion experience toward greater sensitivity and a willingness to prioritize his wife's concerns? How can she believe that he is capable of sustaining such a conversion?

I believe the wife in this counseling scenario represents the feelings of many African-Americans in the U.S.A. They're sick and tired of discussing and debating the same issues again and again. Many have given up and have given in to their frustrations and anger. They are tired of hearing people ask, "Do you think racism still exists today?" or "Why are blacks so angry when you people have come so far?" A fair amount of African-Americans have crossed their arms and shut off their emotions from hoping yet again that significant change will ever be accomplished.

On the other hand, you have many well-meaning whites who have seen the light. Because of Promise Keepers conferences, compelling sermons, critical books on the subject, or exposure through interracial acquaintanceships, their hearts and minds have warmed toward racial reconciliation. A fair amount of whites are on a new journey toward reconciliation. They want to dance but are unsure how. In fact, they are frustrated because whenever they try to come onto the dance floor, they have to figure the moves out on their own. They feel like there is no one to extend a helping hand. That must hurt. And that's exactly how the husband on the couch feels. He is hurt that his wife would not want to work things out after so many years of marriage. Looking over to her, he would cry out, "Sweetheart, what's the problem?" She would fire back, "That's the problem!" The fact that the husband didn't know the problem is a major part of the problem.

The coldness and angry retorts from the wife leave the husband feeling hurt, confused, and frustrated. That's exactly how the white pastor felt after reaching out to the black pastor. He felt like he wasn't being met halfway.

The first step to reconciliation is when both parties know that the other is sincere. The black pastor knew that the white pastor was sincere when he backed up his talk with action. The black pastor needed proof that the white pastor was sincere because there was no desire in his heart or room in his calendar for racial reconciliation games. He needed demonstration that a conversion of attitude would lead to sustained action, that this was not just another opportunity for white guilt to be appeased. The white pastor, on the other hand, needed to know that he wasn't being taken for granted or taken advantage of by the black pastor.

UNDERSTANDING THE FRUSTRATION OF THE BEIGE CULTURES

Although there are no children or any other relatives in the counseling session with the husband and wife, the tension's impact on others who live in their house cannot be ignored. Divorce and division always result in collateral damage. Years of research has shown that children of divorced parents suffer in a myriad of ways. Broken and dysfunctional families often complicate relating patterns and family unity. This is true with racial reconciliation as well. When the bookends of racial reconciliation refuse to move toward each other, others on the shelf are affected. How many Asian store owners and Hispanic witnesses do you think were impacted by the Los Angeles riots in 1992? Surely those victims weren't saying, "Oh well, this was just a black-white issue and I'm not affected." It's quite the contrary. Asians, Latinos, Indians, Native Americans, and many others are relevant to the discussion. The stakes are high for others in America no matter their racial or economic background.

Someone has stated that 70 percent of the world is beige, meaning tan skinned. Much of America is seeing a rise within its borders of the Latino, Middle Eastern, and Asian populations. Each of these groups has its own cultural issues and ethnic priorities that must be incorporated onto our dance floor of ministry. For instance, your church may need to teach English as a second language to Spanish speakers or Spanish as a second language to English speakers.

Speaking of cultural issues and needs, Korean store owners sometimes have been perceived as rude and aloof because they do not look at or acknowledge their customers. However, many Koreans were reared not to look a person in the eye as a sign of submission and respect. Understanding this minor cultural difference can completely change one's perception of rudeness and respect. It can quell frustration and enable conversation so people can begin to build bridges instead of blowing them up.

We all need to improve our sensitivity. In fact, sensitivity is a virtue that I'm constantly learning. For instance, when Amber announced to me that she was pregnant with our first child, it happened to be at the most unfortunate time—right in the middle of a professional football game on television! I was closely following the play by play desecration of my beloved Washington Redskins when she came into the room beaming and said, "Sweetie, guess what?" Did I look up? I wish I had! "I'm pregnant," she exclaimed. I responded, "Great, baby. Let's talk about it after the game." When the game ended, I went upstairs to find my wife so we could celebrate. You can probably guess that Amber was not in the celebrating mood. I felt like a heel. Of course, women readers may say, "You should!" The guys are wondering who won the game. The Redskins were beaten. Amber forgave me. Not all was lost on this extremely emotional day!

(9)

Frustration can lead to anger. Anger can lead to resentment and then bitterness and malice. The Bible has much to say about how Christians should address such frustration and anger. In the next chapter we will address these human behaviors from a biblical perspective that will improve interpersonal relations in general and race relations in particular.

chapter six

THE RACIAL RECONCILIATION MATRIX

I N THE HIT MOVIE *THE MATRIX*, NEO WAS AN ORDI-
nary computer guy living a mundane life until he was whisked
away into a different world. New realities and rules governed this
universe.

What led Neo, played by Keanu Reeves, into this new existence was one critical event: a decision to swallow a blue pill or a
red pill. Choosing the blue pill meant Neo would return to his
normal way of life in his old world of nonexcitement. The red
pill meant going deeper into the new world of the matrix—a
new way of living, thinking, and experiencing—never to return to
the old life.

Neo resolutely made his decision. He swallowed the red pill and
entered a conversion process that changed him forever. He was transformed into a new man who, with a newly programmed mind,
dressed differently and perceived the world with a new set of eyes.
Neo dodged bullets, defied gravity, and experienced instantaneous
information downloads into his brain. He even discovered a new
enemy he had not known existed. The enemy and his cronies were
not human but often cloaked themselves in human form. In time
Neo realized that he had the power, the authority, and new
weaponry to fight these seemingly overpowering enemies. Although
it took a while for Neo to feel comfortable with the new person he
was becoming, over time he grew into the anointed role that fate
had appointed.

SPIRITUAL PARALLELS IN *THE MATRIX*

Do you notice the similarities between this popular film and the journey of the Christian?

Every individual faces a turning point in which he or she must choose whether to follow Jesus as Lord and Savior. The point of decision, although not inaugurated by the swallowing of a pill, is often solidified by a prayer of commitment or some other line of demarcation. Some Christians cannot remember a distinct decision; rather they describe a period of time in which they experienced a process of surrendering to Jesus. Once unbelievers have a born-again experience, whether instantaneous or gradual, a process of development takes place during which the input of Scripture and the exercise of prayer, worship, and submission to the Holy Spirit's control begins to transform the old person into a new person.

Like Neo, we as Christ-followers begin to live in the matrix intersecting the natural world and the spiritual world. Life in the matrix of these two realities is never easy. With the spiritual transformation that accompanies becoming a Christian, the way many of us used to think, act, feel, and process information changes radically. Our hearts as Christ-followers feel differently about sin, and our minds think differently about heaven and earth. The weapons of our warfare are spiritual, and we recognize that our enemy is not made of flesh and blood. The anointed position God has appointed for us is not easily realized without setting our minds to it, and on Christ!

By the time the sequels, *The Matrix Reloaded* and *The Matrix Revolutions*, hit theaters, Neo was comfortable with his new powers in his new world. Having to learn how to dance between punches and bullets like never before, his body moved at paces and in places unimagined. Is this not also true of Christians who practice the dance of living between heaven and earth? We need to learn to live well *in* the world without being *of* the world. Practicing the dance of Christianity while living in two worlds is a task that requires help from God. Not only is this true of living the Christian life, but our need for God's help becomes more evident when we try to live as reconcilers.

Reconciliation in any form, no matter the style of dance, requires a spiritually transformed mind with transformed members of one's body. To relate at high levels of acceptance and grace with people who are different than you takes a heart fully surrendered to the Holy Spirit.

Without the Spirit's supernatural presence and influence in our lives, we often practice cordiality and tolerance instead of love and acceptance. Levels of true communion where groups of diverse people dance in unity can be experienced only by those who have entered into the Holy Spirit's matrix through a relationship with the Lord Jesus Christ. Our frustration factors, as discussed in the last chapter, can leave us with attitudes and disappointments that must be submitted to the control of the Spirit's power. Otherwise, the residue of negative racial attitudes, bad feelings, and unfortunate racial experiences can sabotage what Christians were appointed to be and do as ambassadors of reconciliation.

The apostle Paul explains the two-world phenomenon quite convincingly in the third chapter of Colossians. Allow me to explain the passage in such a way that we can learn together what attitudes and actions should accompany our relational efforts as we dance in two worlds—the natural and spiritual. I like to call this the Racial Reconciliation Matrix.

IDENTITY (WHO WE ARE)

As you view the top left quadrant of the diagram (p. 76), see how Paul addresses issues of Christian identity in the form of five statements. I have arranged these identity statements in progressive order.

Identity

- Died to self
- Raised with him
- Seated with him
- Life in Jesus Christ
- Appear with him

THE RACIAL RECONCILIATION MATRIX

Colossians 3

[1]Since, then, you have been raised with Christ, set your hearts on things above, where Christ is seated at the right hand of God. [2]Set your minds on things above, not on earthly things. [3]For you died, and your life is now hidden with Christ in God. [4]When Christ, who is your life, appears, then you also will appear with him in glory.

[5]Put to death, therefore, whatever belongs to your earthly nature: sexual immorality, impurity, lust, evil desires and greed, which is idolatry. [6]Because of these, the wrath of God is coming. [7]You used to walk in these ways, in the life you once lived. [8]But now you must rid yourselves of all such things as these: anger, rage, malice, slander, and filthy language from your lips. [9]Do not lie to each other, since you have taken off your old self with its practices [10]and have put on the new self, which is being renewed in knowledge in the image of its Creator. [11]Here there is no Greek or Jew, circumcised or uncircumcised, barbarian, Scythian, slave or free, but Christ is all, and is in all.

[12]Therefore, as God's chosen people, holy and dearly loved, clothe your-selves with compassion, kindness, humility, gentleness and patience. [13]Bear with each other and forgive whatever grievances you may have against one another. Forgive as the Lord forgave you. [14]And over all these virtues put on love, which binds them all together in perfect unity.

Identity

- Died to self
- Raised with him
- Seated with him
- Life in Jesus Christ
- Appear with him

Idolatry

- Sexual immorality
- Impurity
- Lust
- Evil desires
- Greed

Old Clothes

- Anger
- Rage
- Malice
- Slander
- Filthy language

New Clothes

- Compassion
- Kindness
- Humility
- Gentleness
- Patience

Practical Application

- Bear with each other
- Forgive each other
- Love each other

Identity Factor 1: We died to self (Col. 3:3)

When Christians want to parade their personal freedoms, rights, and special interests, they must always yield the right of way to the Lordship of Christ. Our emotions, desires, fears, stereotypes, history, or cultural priorities must take a back seat to the driving force of God's Word regardless of how we feel.

How do you think race relations within the church would change if this were the driving force of all of our decisions regarding budgets, locations, music, and the choice of small-group members?

Identity Factor 2: We are raised with Christ (Col. 3:1)

An important factor in understanding our identity in Christ is remembering that we have been raised with him, meaning that the power and position of the resurrected Christ is ours. We must understand that we can tap into the power of the resurrection, as Paul longed for in Philippians 3:10 when he said, "I want to know Christ and the power of his resurrection." Then we can rest in the fact that our feet need not be bolted to earth in such a way that we become racially, politically, or culturally imprisoned.

I met a racially mixed woman at a church function. She confessed that she often felt confused and, at times, like a second-class citizen. Having grown up during the days of forced segregation in the United States—often faced with choices such as whether to ride the black bus or the white bus for a school field trip—she questioned who, or even what, she was. However, after she became a follower of Christ and learned that she had been raised with Christ, her identity took on different meaning. While she still had to work through her issues of identity as a human, she began to understand the deep spiritual truth that she had been raised with Christ and that her ultimate identity is in the one who created her.

Identity Factor 3: We are seated with Christ (Col. 3:1)

Have you ever noticed the correlation between authority and the concept of being seated? One December evening, a forty-two-year-old seamstress left work and boarded a bus for home. She was tired. But this was Montgomery, Alabama, in 1955. So as the bus filled, this black woman was ordered to give up her seat in the black section of the crowded bus to a white passenger. Rosa Parks's simple decision to refuse to relinquish her seat became a watershed moment that eventually led to the disintegration of institutionalized segregation in the South. I believe that the issue was greater than a weary working woman refusing to stand so that a white person could sit. When you think about it, Rosa Parks's seat on the bus represented a symbolic struggle for authority.

In Western culture, attorneys in court stand to address judges who are seated in a position of power. The president of the United States may be referred to as the person in the "seat of power." Kings sit on their thrones as petitioners or advisers stand at their feet. When American troops toppled Baghdad during the war in 2003, they entered into one of Saddam Hussein's many palaces and marched into the inner sanctum. They sat in Saddam's throne of power, signifying their abduction of his authority.

The Bible speaks of elders seated at the gate (see Prov. 31:23), demonstrating that those in authority sat down in the administration of power. In Revelation 4 the Lord is seated on his throne with twenty-four elders seated on other thrones.

What Colossians is telling us is that we have been seated with Christ in the ultimate position of authority, a position that was conferred, not usurped. God has invested in all of us as believers a high position of power that should embolden us to rise above the petty preoccupations of racial prejudices and worldly skirmishes that, if we're not careful, will suck us into the quagmire of low self-esteem and identity confusion.

Identity Factor 4: Our life is in Christ (Col. 3:4)

Not only have we died to ourselves, been raised with Christ, and been seated with him, but Paul tells us that our very life is in Christ (Col. 3:4).

Elsewhere in Scripture the apostle says that for him "to live is Christ" (Phil. 1:21). We have all been crucified with Christ; it is no longer we who live but Christ lives through us (Gal. 2:20). As believers our very lives are enveloped by Christ. Jesus is our identity. He is our life. All that you and I say and do should reflect Jesus Christ shining through us from the inside out.

Can you imagine the impact on the body of Christ if black and white and beige Christians lived this truth out in their church policies, social policies, and evangelism efforts? Imagine doing evangelism as if Christ is living through you to others. Such evangelism would be elevated from speaking the good news alone to demonstrating the good news as Christ shines through your everyday living, serving, and loving.

I witnessed such an expression of Christlikeness shining through a Christian white man named Mike. Whenever he heard that Jesse, an older black man, needed an oil change or some other service done on his car, Mike would drive to Jesse's house and work under the hood. A relationship developed as Mike continually served Jesse with the heart of Christ.

Mike didn't know Jesse's background. He didn't know that Jesse had experienced years of fighting corporate glass ceilings and systematic discrimination. He didn't know Jesse struggled with his attitude toward white people.

An African-American friend invited Jesse to our multicultural church without informing him that the church was multicultural. On the Sunday of Jesse's first visit, one of my associate pastors, a Caucasian man, was preaching. Jesse turned around and walked out of the church. Later he told his buddy, "I have to live around and work with white people; the last place I want to be with them is in church. It is my only place of solace with black folks. Don't make me worship with them too."

However, after several weeks passed, Jesse's attitude began to change. Jesse confided to me that the pain of discrimination was slowly healing because of white people like Mike. Jesse went on to say that every time he gets angry with the "white system" at work, he reminds himself that not all whites are that way. He no longer feels like he needs the traditional black church to comfort him or fan the flames of his anger.

Jesse became an elder at our church and a major proponent of racial reconciliation. It all began with a person like Mike, just letting Christ live through him—the first step toward breaking down barriers of hurt and history.

Identity Factor 5: We will appear with Christ (Col. 3:4)

Finally, in this first quadrant, we are encouraged to remember that the phenomenon of dual living will come to an end. We will appear with Christ in the last day as he wraps up his business on the earth and ushers all believers into the eternal state, where there no longer will be the old earth with its sinful dilemmas, divisions, and dangers. People from every tribe and nation will appear together as one happy family around the throne of the one who is our ultimate authority and the object of our multicultural worship.

While the first set of verses in the upper left quadrant instruct us on who we are in Christ, focusing on our identity as a believer, the next set of verses instruct us on who we are not, focusing on idolatry.

IDOLATRY (WHO WE ARE NOT)

The upper right quadrant of the Racial Reconciliation Matrix lists another category of five things Paul says must be addressed.

The behaviors in verse 5 are identified as idolatry. In other words, if you are a believer and understand your identity in Christ as explained in verses 1 through 4, Paul wants you to be sure that you are clear that any lifestyle apart from your identity as a Christian is serving another god and should be seen as idolatry. Paul says that believers in Jesus

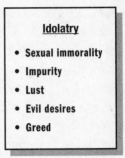

Idolatry

- **Sexual immorality**
- **Impurity**
- **Lust**
- **Evil desires**
- **Greed**

must consider five idolatrous behaviors as dead in their everyday lives: sexual immorality, impurity, lust, evil desires, and greed. These sinful patterns belong to the earthly nature and the old way of life. The above list of sinful behaviors is normal for unbelievers but abnormal for believers who are living in their identity as true Christians. The wrath of God is coming on all idolaters, or those who have not chosen Christ as Savior. But remember, you took the red pill. Like Neo, you made a life-changing decision you can't go back on. You chose Christ and he has transformed your life. Therefore, consider the old way of life dead.

Ponder this question: Which of the two lists, the two upper quadrants, represents the perspective and pattern of your life? Paul is showing us two different kinds of people, the old and the new. The new person whose life is submitted to Christ must begin to live in the perspective of the upper left quadrant. The old person whose life has not been submitted to Christ is still living in the upper right quadrant, without conviction, confession, or cleansing.

OLD CLOTHES

The bottom left quadrant of the Racial Reconciliation Matrix lists normal behaviors Paul says the old person engages in. Using the language of clothing to communicate his point, he shows the Colossians that they have been delivered from the old way of idolatrous

living and must therefore take off the old
clothing, namely, anger, rage, malice, slander,
and filthy language. This old clothing represents the old person. However, with a new
person and a new identity comes new clothing or behavior.

Old Clothes

- Anger
- Rage
- Malice
- Slander
- Filthy language

To be honest, I struggle with many of
the items in the upper right quadrant and
the bottom left quadrant (idolatry and old clothes). Maybe you
do too. But the encouraging thing about this passage is that it
reminds us of who we are in Christ and who we are not! We are
reminded by this passage that we are first and foremost children
of God. Race, class, culture, social status, denomination, and so on,
are all secondary to this one truth. I do my best to crucify my old
person and strip off my old clothing. Is it not helpful to know that
we are not told simply to take off the old clothes but that God
has provided us with new clothing to wear?

NEW CLOTHES

New Clothes

- Compassion
- Kindness
- Humility
- Gentleness
- Patience

In Colossians 3:12, Paul lists one more
category of five items. Notice in the bottom
right quadrant of the matrix diagram the new
clothes believers are instructed to wear. The
verse says that we are God's "chosen people,"
reminding us of our identity and that we are
to "clothe" ourselves with five qualities: compassion, kindness,
humility, gentleness, and patience.

What a tall order for anyone! If you can affirm that as a Christian you have died to yourself, are raised with Christ, are seated
with him, live in him, and will appear with him, then you are commanded to behave with compassion. This means to act mercifully
toward others. You and I are also commanded to be kind, a quality

often demonstrated through our words. We are to be humble by rightly viewing ourselves in relation to God and others. We are to be gentle in our treatment of others, and patient, waiting on God to act or waiting on others to grow as we keep ourselves at peace and emotionally steady. These are the clothes of the new person whose life is in Christ.

Sometimes I use my lunch hour to play basketball at a local gym. After several games I will drag my sweaty self off the court and into the locker room to shower and get dressed before I return to work. Can you imagine if I returned to work without a shower? Whoosh. My coworkers would realize in just a short time that there is a fungus among us.

I think this is what it must be like for unbelievers (upper right quadrant) to try to wear the new clothes (bottom right quadrant) of believers. Although non-Christians can be compassionate and kind, the real person shows through after a while. In time, the fungus of fleshly living, ungodly behavior, and selfish motivations surfaces. It takes the Holy Spirit to make the new clothes fit. However, Paul's point to the Colossians would be more analogous to my taking a shower at the gym after playing basketball and then putting my grungy gym clothes back on. Now that's gross! That's Paul's point. The old clothes of anger, rage, malice, slander, and filthy language should feel gross to believers who have been cleansed by Christ.

These five behaviors seem to be par for the course when dealing with race relations in the world. Within the church of Jesus Christ, this should not be. According to the Colossians 3 matrix, believers who are identified with Christ (upper left quadrant) are to wear new clothes and act in new ways (bottom right quadrant). Wouldn't it be great if Christians could bridge the racial divide within the church by living the new clothes philosophy when addressing race issues?

PRACTICAL APPLICATION

Paul doesn't end this section of Scripture without giving a few practical words to help us. In verse 11, we are reminded that we are one in Christ and that there is no division based on race or status in Jesus. And it is based on this equality of high calling and common identification that Paul exhorts the Colossians to handle their differences by doing three things:

1. *Bear with each other (v. 13):* We are to put up with and suffer long each other's differences out of our reverence for Christ. It is helpful to know that even for the New Testament Christians, reconciliation wasn't a cakewalk. There were differences that they had to just endure.

2. *Forgive each other (v. 13):* Paul didn't simply say forgive each other and move on. A blanket acceptance of wrongdoing is not his command. He seems to be saying it is necessary to deal with grievances and offenses. There are specific acts and attitudes that need to be brought to the surface for repentance. Then we must "forgive as the Lord forgave you."

3. *Love each other (v. 14):* Love is the virtue that ties everything together in perfect unity. Love calls us to a higher level of selflessness than any other virtue. Love is the ultimate act that bridges the great divide between God and human beings. Such love is personified by the death, burial, and resurrection of Jesus Christ. This kind of love for one another is what it will take for believers to be true ambassadors of reconciliation.

In one of our racial reconciliation small groups at Bridgeway, I went over the matrix of Colossians 3 and allowed the group to tease truth out of the text as it relates to racial reconciliation. As we enter a new section of the book, I will show in the next chapter the practical ways in which Colossians 3 came to life within our small group.

part 3

THE PRACTICAL GROOVE

chapter seven

GROOVING WITH SMALL GROUPS

A S A FATHER OF YOUNG CHILDREN, I HAVE SAT through many animated movies. I've watched so many that I could go on for hours discussing the best animated films of the last few years. (I won't.) Remember *The Emperor's New Groove*? It's the story of a selfish king hated by his subjects. One night he drinks a badly mixed potion that, instead of killing him as the poisoner wanted, turns him into a llama. The film tells how the llama-king seeks to be transformed back to human royalty. During the process he realizes that building a utopian kingdom for his own glory upon the backs of his underlings is wrong. Fast-forward to the end of the story. What happens? The llama-king is returned to human form, this time with a new groove, a new mind-set. The emperor's new groove makes him someone his people want to follow.

STARTING THE JOURNEY TOWARD GETTING A NEW GROOVE

In the last chapter I mentioned that Colossians 3 came to life for me in one of the racial reconciliation small groups I facilitated. We found ourselves on a journey toward getting a new groove. The emotional and spiritual (and in some cases political and social) places where people found themselves when they started the group were not the same places they found themselves after participating in the groups. Since then, many racial reconciliation groups have grown out of our church.

We got started by meeting a couple of times to discuss the following introductory questions:

1. What should our objective or purpose as a group on the topic of racial reconciliation be?
2. What do you hope will be accomplished for you personally by the end of the group?
3. What should our timeline be?
4. What should our rules of discussion be?
5. What themes do you think will or should dominate our discussions?

After these discussions, the group began to get into a rhythm. While it was awkward at first, once the group began to formulate its purpose, everyone felt a sense of shared ownership. The group settled on this purpose statement: To develop a deeper understanding and a greater respect for each other as we implement practical approaches to racial reconciliation. As a reminder, I printed this statement at the top of every handout I distributed in each session. Let's take a closer look at the three-pronged purpose statement.

1. Develop deeper understanding. The group recognized that their understanding of each other was limited. The group had five men and five women. Five were black. Five were white. Three of the whites were Jewish. Ages ranged from twenty-four to fifty-four years. (At this time in our church's history we had few Asians and Latinos. Now, 13 percent of our church is made up of Asians, Latinos, and other ethnic groups.)

2. Develop greater respect. Although we didn't see any signs of disrespect, it was important to this group to verbalize their desire to learn. Some had a general respect for those who were different but not an intelligent respect based on experiential knowledge. They truly wanted to understand each other.

One evening I asked the group to divide up and list their perceptions of what it was like to grow up as the other race. An interesting "aha" moment occurred when we reassembled. The black members said that growing up as a white person in America was like growing up with a silver spoon in one's mouth. In response, one white woman shared her story of growing up in the dysfunctional home of divorced parents. As she went on to share her difficulties, another white person jumped in to share his upbringing. It also was anything but silver spoon. One black woman's mouth dropped and she said, "I would not have ever known. I'm really sorry." That night I knew that deeper respect for one another was growing.

3. *Develop practical approaches.* In many ways, this group set their own rules, or music so to speak, for what were acceptable dance steps. They were by no means waltzing, but at least they were on the same dance floor moving to the same music. In my mind, this was a small win.

CONTINUING THE JOURNEY

At the end of our time together, this group wanted to know how they could utilize the information they would learn from one another to continue their journey of reconciliation. It was important for them to feel they could get a handle on the topic and learn how to move in and out of it with greater ease than when they entered the group. To help the process, I introduced them to the Colossians 3 matrix. Then I had them break into groups by race to answer the following questions:

> *Whites:* What grievances do you perceive whites may have with blacks regarding the issue of race?
>
> *Blacks:* What grievances do you perceive blacks may have with whites regarding the issue of race?

I phrased the questions in terms of grievances that races as a whole might have rather than grievances that individuals in the group might have in case someone wasn't ready to self-disclose. That way everyone could feel comfortable participating because they weren't revealing how they felt personally.

The two small groups spent about thirty minutes in discussion, and then I called the groups together. I wrote the list of grievances on a white board for everyone to see. Then I reread the Colossians 3 passage. After noting the Practical Applications portion of the matrix— bearing with each other, forgiving each other, and loving each other— I asked the following three questions:

1. Which grievances must both communities bear with as we walk together?
2. Which grievances need forgiveness applied?
3. How can love be expressed by both communities?

Answers to these questions from the black group ranged from insensitivity and negative stereotypes to assimilation, discrimination, and equality issues. Some were ready to give up on reconciliation and turn toward afrocentrism. Others even spoke of returning to the exclusively black church experience.

The white group came up with statements like, "Blacks just want to be with their own kind," and, "Blacks have a chip on their shoulder." Some whites implored blacks to stop with the "all whites are guilty of racism until proven innocent" mentality, while others said that "blacks need to do something and quit whining."

I'm sure you can imagine how interesting the discussion became when these statements were written on the board. It was as if the music for interracial dancing came to a screeching halt. I allowed each group to respond to the grievances of the other to see what kind of responses surfaced. Some whites responded, "We need you to believe the best and stop assuming the worst about us. We're not all racists!" Some blacks responded, "Why don't you believe that racism is still a problem instead of just dismissing what we say as whining?"

After an hour we came to some conclusions. One was that each person in the group needed a "reconciliation buddy." We exchanged phone numbers and committed to walking and talking together throughout our time as a group.

We also decided that each person needed to listen to their reconciliation buddy's race story. It was wonderful to see people getting to know others from a different background. By the end of the six weeks we were together, the participants bonded to such a degree that they didn't want the group to end. It was as if someone turned up the dancing music and no one wanted to stop the dance. The group members began making arrangements to get together to share experiences such as attending the Holocaust Museum in Washington, D.C., and viewing certain movies. It was evident that these believers were bearing with each other and learning how to love one another. I trust that over time some of them even learned how to forgive one another.

RACIAL RECONCILIATION SMALL-GROUP CURRICULUM

Several years ago, while completing a graduate degree, I sought to verify that small group experiences could positively influence racial attitudes. I embarked on a project I titled "The Development of a Racial Reconciliation Model for Ministry," specifically utilizing the small group model as a testing ground for teaching reconciliation. I had a hunch that going to church together was not enough to bring about reconciliation. I suspect you would agree. My premise was that attitudes could be positively influenced if people could just interact with others from different racial backgrounds while studying the truth of Scripture in a group setting.

The purpose of the project was to facilitate racial reconciliation between black and white Christians in my church while providing a ministry model and curriculum for other churches. Including other racial groups in my study would have been too much research to handle, so I was encouraged to pare it down to two groups. I chose the bookends—whites and blacks. My objectives were:

1. To create honest dialogue between both groups
2. To provide a safe group in which understanding can be sought

3. To facilitate the process of relationship-building
4. To facilitate a process of introspection, in which each
    individual can assess their prejudices, attitudes, and sins
    for the purpose of personal repentance
5. To provide each individual with the tools to continue
    their journey of reconciliation after the group has ended
6. To cultivate within each individual a vision to become an
    ambassador of reconciliation as they journey into the
    future

I placed an announcement in the church bulletin for anyone
interested in participating in a six-week study. I accepted twenty
people and divided them into two small groups. Here are the steps
we took:

1. After contacting each person, I sent a survey of racial
    attitudes to each of them to be collected prior to our
    first meeting. (See appendix 1.)
2. Based on their answers, I devised a six-session, small-
    group curriculum. (See appendix 2.) The first three
    weeks of the study focused on racism. I believed, and
    still hold, that reconciliation cannot be adequately han-
    dled without a clear understanding of racism.
3. After completing the six sessions, I gave each member a
    survey similar to the first.
4. After comparing the surveys from both groups and com-
    paring the results, my premise was confirmed. Statisti-
    cally speaking, racial attitudes were significantly more
    positive after the six weeks. The experience was memo-
    rable and I found the research invaluable.

CONCLUSION

Remember Jesse, the African-American man who walked out of our church when he visited for the first time because a Caucasian man was speaking? Do you recall what convinced him to stop running away from our church and to become an elder? It was a white man named Mike—and many others, I might add—who turned the tide of Jesse's opinions about all whites by serving Jesse as Jesus would. One of the most beautiful things about this groundbreaking small-group project was not just the statistical values or the attitude adjustments. Guess who opened his home to host the small group? That's right, Jesse!

At one point Jesse didn't even want to be in the same church with white folk, but now, because of worshiping and building relationships with whites, Jesse opened his home to the very subject that had caused so much turmoil in the past. This is the power of multicultural ministry. It's the church's new groove, and Jesse is now in step.

Each member in the small group was able to evaluate what he or she believed about race and whether he or she was part of the problem or part of the solution. In the next chapter, I will help you discover what side of the race problem you may find yourself on. My hope is that by the end of this book you will find yourself—if you're not already there—on the solution side.

chapter eight

THE RACIAL RECONCILIATION CONTINUUM

ARE YOU A RACIST? ARE YOU A RECONCILER? OR ARE you somewhere in between?

In my work as a consultant on race relations, I have discovered that without the assistance of definitions, it's difficult to identify whether one is a racist or reconciler. In one of my racial reconciliation small groups, I decided to develop a continuum chart with which people could identify where they stood in their attitudes. The exercise was quite revealing for the group and may be for you as well.

In creating the Racial Reconciliation Continuum, I paralleled the continuum of faith commonly used in evangelism. In evangelism you can assess people's readiness to hear the gospel by identifying them as atheist, cynic, agnostic, or seeker. After a person has converted, he or she is identified as a new believer, also known as a babe in Christ. As the Christian babe grows, he or she becomes a young child, a teen, an adult, and then a mature believer.

You can see the parallels between the continuum of faith and the racial reconciliation continuum in the diagram.

RACIAL RECONCILIATION CONTINUUM

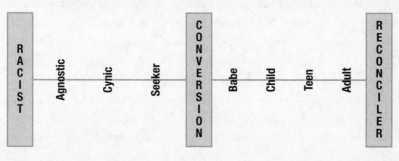

THE CONTINUUM

On the far left of the continuum is *the racist*. A racist harbors ill feelings, and possibly hatred, toward a particular group of people because of color, class, or culture. Such feelings cause that person to speak, act, or think negatively toward or about this group.

The middle of the continuum is the point of racial-reconciliation conversion. Conversion is the point in, let's say, a woman's life when she realizes that God wants her to deal with issues of race in her own heart or in society. She awakens to the knowledge that things are desperately wrong. She realizes that God desires her to make a difference first personally and then in society. Such enlightenment may occur as a result of friendships, sermons, conferences, books, classes, or some impressionable experience. Positive experiences like a missions trip can be eye opening, as can negative experiences like being victimized by acts of racial hatred.

Between the racist and the point of conversion are agnostics, cynics, and seekers. An *agnostic* doesn't really care about other races or racial issues. He is happy being with his own kind. A *cynic* is pessimistic about real change truly occurring and is unwilling to seek out change or make concerted efforts. A *seeker* is somewhat ignorant about other races or racial issues but is willing to learn and desires to grow in this new area.

On the far right of the continuum is *the reconciler*. The reconciler is a person fully devoted to being a change agent. He understands that God has called him to be an ambassador of reconciliation. This person accepts the call by seeking to educate himself on race relations and is developing cross-cultural relationships. He seeks to be a channel of God's love, grace, justice, and forgiveness through friendships and societal contributions. A reconciler is a reproducer, a teacher who finds innovative ways to build bridges for others to walk across.

A person who has reached the point of conversion and is ready to move along the continuum will go through four stages of growth:

babe, child, teen, adult. A *babe* is newly born in her awareness of racial issues and has come to realize that she needs to deal with issues of race relations in order to be all that God has called us to be as reconcilers. A babe depends on others to help feed her and lead her in the new area of racial reconciliation. A *child* is a young and growing learner who is active in ascertaining knowledge regarding race while trying to apply new information. The child is energetic and excited but lacks discernment when applying the new knowledge in everyday relationships. A *teen* is developing and maturing in the area of reconciliation. The teen is steadily building bridges of reconciliation while periodically failing in doing so. He is winning at times and losing at times as he struggles through the issues and relationships of reconciliation. An *adult* is active in taking responsibility as a reconciler and contributes where she can to make reconciliation happen. The adult is more than a bridge-builder who is still growing and learning; she has become a bridge-leader in that she is far enough ahead to help others to convert and grow. She is a dedicated reproducer.

Where are you on the continuum? Based on these definitions, can you see more clearly where you are and where you need to go?

MOVING ALONG THE CONTINUUMS

Anthony was a non-Christian who began visiting our men's ministry, which we called the MOB, or the Men of Bridgeway. After several Saturdays of visiting, Anthony was ready to make the big step of attending a Sunday morning service. To his pleasant surprise, the church met him where he was spiritually. In an attempt to build a bridge, I invited Anthony to lunch. Several days later, as we sat across from one another at a café, Anthony and I transitioned from small talk to more spiritually significant matters, like—race cars! But after thoroughly discussing engines we moved toward the topic of race. He wanted me to know that he doubted Christ and that he doubted the success of a church that was proactively mixing the races.

"Do you think it will work, David?" he inquired.

"Will what work?" I asked him.

"Having a church with whites and others," he said.

I emphatically said yes and explained my vision of what the love of Christ could look like.

Anthony was a seeker on both the continuum of faith and the continuum of racial reconciliation. I had not witnessed this parallel track so clearly before. As Anthony, an African-American, began seeking the truth about Christ, he was also processing his doubts and pain about those who have misused that same faith. It was a fascinating barrier to overcome. The good news is that after weeks of regular meetings at the café and several visits to our multicultural church, Anthony gave his life to Christ. While moving on the continuum of faith, Anthony also moved on the continuum of racial reconciliation. He was in one of my very first racial reconciliation small groups. In fact, you'll never guess what Anthony's favorite passage of Scripture is—Colossians 3!

THE CONTINUUM AS A DIAGNOSTIC TOOL

I recall using the reconciliation continuum in a forum of about fifty administrators during a weekend retreat. These college presidents, deans, and recruiters had all read my book, *Letters across the Divide*, prior to the weekend. After I had the administrators mark their spot on the continuum, I used colored markers on a white board to show where on the continuum they stood as a group. Most of the marks were clustered to the right of the conversion point between teen and adult. I then had each administrator mark the spot where he or she believed the majority of their faculty to be. And then I had them repeat the exercise for their student bodies.

We discovered something very interesting. Because the administrators were attending a retreat on the subject, it was really no surprise that the majority of them marked themselves toward the right side of the continuum. Their student bodies were pretty far to the right as well. But most of the administrators marked their faculty at agnostic or cynic, to the far left of the conversion point.

I then asked the administrators a few questions. "Who do you think has the most influence on the minds and lives of the students in your institution? Who do you think will shape the ministries of the church of tomorrow, the faculty or the administration?"

There was a sense of "aha" in the room, and then a sense of "oh no," and then "hmm?" The administrators began thinking through the negative effects of having faculty members on the racist side of the continuum while the rest of society was moving toward reconciliation. They left the weekend knowing they had some challenges to face.

The continuum was a simple yet effective tool that helped these educational leaders evaluate themselves and their organizations. Now the test for the administrators was to discern the best method to close the gap between faculty, administration, and students.

CONCLUSION

I enjoy consulting because I get to ask the tough questions and then leave. The most difficult part of running an organization is knowing the right questions to ask and then figuring out how to strategically move the organization toward stated goals. I hope you will take the time to place yourself on the continuum and then prayerfully think through how you can move forward. Progression will almost always require more education through reading, listening to alternative sources of information, and building relationships with those who are of a different background. Placing yourself in areas where such relationships can be built is critical. This may mean you will have to change where you shop, work out, buy gas, or play soccer. Reconciliation takes intentionality. If God were not intentional, Jesus would have never come to Earth to be our bridge of reconciliation.

Churches, colleges, and other organizations must follow God's pattern. They must strategize if they desire to build bridges of reconciliation. I remember how difficult it was to find successful models for doing multicultural ministry when I started my church in Maryland just over a decade ago. Wouldn't it be great if in the decade to come the continuum were used in small groups, Bible study groups, Sunday school classes, board meetings, committee meetings, seminars, and workshops as a tool for racial reconciliation? Nothing would make me happier.

Because there are still few models for multicultural ministry, in the next chapter I will assist leaders in strategizing ways to get their church or organization in the reconciliation groove. I call these leaders groove strategists.

chapter nine

GROOVE STRATEGISTS

IKE DEEJAYS, CHURCH LEADERS TURN THE KNOBS ON the racial sound boards of their organizations. A church leader knows when there's too much talk about race and when there is not enough. A church leader knows when the core value of racial reconciliation is lagging behind the other core values within their ministry.

The church leader also has the responsibility of balancing the different sounds of race. For example, when we started Bridgeway Community Church it was mainly a biracial church, black and white. We launched it with a predominately white leadership group, about 90 percent white. I knew that once the word spread that a young African-American male was starting a new and innovative ministry in town, African-Americans would come in droves. In our fifth year of ministry, our racial mix was approximately 54 percent black, 39 percent white, and 7 percent other. After our tenth year we surveyed our mix again. Bridgeway is now about 55–60 percent black, 30 percent white, and 12 percent other.

Ethnic groups flock, which is why the "other" category, mainly Latinos and Asians, has grown into double digits. Looking at our numbers, one might think that over the last five years we were losing whites. But what we learned was that we gain nonwhite growth at a faster rate.

THE FLOCKING PRINCIPLE

Let's say a white visitor and a black visitor attend church on the same Sunday, and both thoroughly enjoy the service. We have learned that the black person will more likely return bringing another visitor, and more quickly, than the white person. This is not because the white guest isn't as excited about the service or as committed to sharing his new church experience. Rather, blacks, Asians, and Latinos in our area have larger family networks. Whites may have only a few family members, a network of business associates, and neighbors to share their new experience with. Also, most likely whites will not receive a high number of positive responses from those they share their church experience with. More likely they'll hear something like a "that's nice for you" comment.

Even non-Christians who are African-Americans tend to have positive affiliations with church. They may call church irrelevant, but they respect it. In fact, they view it as a place to visit where a good time will be had by all. In contrast, while many whites may agree that church is a waste of time, they also may approach it with apprehension. Not that all whites are unchurched or church-phobic; they are uncertain of what they will experience if they attend a denominationally different, and especially "culturally different," church. They are afraid of being offended, "guilted" into giving money, embarrassed, or cornered into conversion. I also have found that many whites who visit Bridgeway face a greater risk of earning family disdain and of being labeled a holy roller or a born-again Jesus freak, especially if they come from Catholic backgrounds.

THE ART OF DEEJAYING

If a deejay is playing music in a club, he may take requests from the audience to discern what genre of music interests them. He may try different styles to test which draws more dancers to the floor. Likewise, church leaders who want to sustain a healthy multicultural body must become groove specialists.

This is what I mean. The preacher must use appropriate analogies and illustrations during the sermon. The director of church education must know when to introduce new material into the curriculum that stretches students in cultural areas. The producers of the Sunday morning service must elevate particular minority groups to visible positions so that others from that group can identify more readily with the church.

Here's an example of how the art of deejaying has worked at Bridgeway. As a groove strategist I was aware that we needed more Asians involved on stage and throughout the church. One of my associate pastors introduced me to a spiritually mature Korean brother in the Lord with whom he had an informal relationship. Kwang Chul Whang, or K. C., as we call him, was a real estate agent in our county and a major connector within the Korean community. We talked with K. C. about making Bridgeway Community Church his family's home for the purpose of participating in multicultural ministry. Within a short time, the Whang family fit right in to the mix at Bridgeway. We introduced K. C. and his wife, Dong, who was also spiritually mature, to be key players in the church and involved them in service in any way we could. We were very clear with the Whang family that though we valued their contribution to multicultural ministry, we wanted the church to be a place where they could be served, loved, and nurtured themselves.

Accepting the challenge to assist with Asian development in the church, Dong became an usher at the front door. K. C. frequented the stage by doing the community news and communion. They both accepted posts as deacons, and they have taken on the responsibility of hosting meetings for Asians in the church who desire to meet the pastors and discuss their journeys.

This plan is a perfect example of groove strategy. If I want Asians on the dance floor of multicultural ministry of Bridgeway, I cannot simply wish them into existence. Playing their music, elevating people who represent them, and showing examples of their lives and culture from the stage is critical to success.

While some may be bothered by what they see as some form of affirmative action, I see it as simply affirming. I see it as respecting, valuing, and including other cultures. I see it as *gracism*—positively giving grace because of race. Such effort has been very beneficial for many of the non-Asians in our church as well. Cross-cultural relationships within our church as a result of the Asian population's presence have been rich and positive.

One day K. C. told me how warmed his heart was when one of my staff members invited his family to dinner. When the Whangs arrived, the hosts' three-year-old African-American daughter greeted them in Korean. The Whangs were floored.

Friends, such relational connections don't happen naturally within the church. Groove strategists think about how to create environments in which such multicultural connections can take place. In this case, a white associate pastor intentionally built a relationship with a Korean businessman. After that businessman connected to the church, his family was welcomed with open arms and involved in ministry. Through the visibility of the Whangs, more Asians began to attend, connect, and get involved. Non-Asians began connecting with the Whangs, resulting in multiple benefits—including a little black girl learning Korean at age three.

PREACHING AND TEACHING

Another groove move that multicultural churches must consider is how to communicate God's Word. Paul told Timothy to preach and teach the Word. I admit that the following statement is a huge generalization, but I have noticed that white churches focus on "teaching the Word" and black churches focus on "preaching the Word." Good multicultural churches do both.

Teaching focuses on information; preaching focuses on inspiration. Around Bridgeway we say that we teach for learning but we preach for living. We have found that whites, generally speaking, like information. If they don't feel like they've learned something, then church, while it may have been a nice experience, wasn't the best way to spend their time. Blacks, on the other hand, generally speaking, prefer inspiration. If they don't feel like they've been motivated to act or respond, then the message, while it may have been good, was not moving. My comments must be taken as generalizations because there are many blacks who want information and whites who want inspiration. But I think the trends are broadly true.

Another interesting insight involves Latinos and Asians. Bridgeway's Hispanic attenders tend to react similarly to the way blacks do. They prefer preaching that inspires. Asians tend to react similarly to whites, preferring teaching. This may explain why Asians tend to integrate more easily into white churches and why Latino and African-American church expression is similiar.

As the senior pastor, I preach about 65 percent of the time. My communication style is viewed as preaching with practical teaching elements within the message. The remaining 35 percent of the time is taken by the other speakers on my team, which consists of one Latino, three whites, and a black. Thus Bridgeway enjoys a plethora of preaching and teaching styles.

For many blacks, attending a white church is much like my French food restaurant date. Let me explain. When Amber and I were first dating, she wanted to expose me to a nice French culinary experience. She treated me to a romantic candlelight meal at a quaint restaurant down the street from the Moody Bible Institute in Chicago, where we were studying at the time. Everything was exquisite. But after we walked out of the restaurant, I greatly disappointed Amber by asking her if she would mind if we stopped somewhere on the way back to our dorms to get a burger. Since then I have learned to be more diplomatic. But the point is that tasty French food wasn't enough to fill me. Have you ever eaten at a French restaurant? The portions are small. At least they're just too small for this 6 foot, 3 inch black man!

Some people leave church wanting more of a spiritual meal than they got. I have heard many blacks say after visiting white churches that church was nice, but they still haven't "had church." For many blacks, church is a verb, not a noun. Church is not just a place where you go but something you have. Black folk can be in a parking lot or at a store or in a car and have church, meaning that whenever they begin to speak about the Lord together and they start to feel something in their fellowship, they are having church. Church is not only a place but an action. Participation is an important part of worship for many African-Americans. In other words, some blacks are still hungry for more after attending white churches, like I was after my French meal.

Whites, on the other hand, might describe a visit to a traditional black church as an interesting experience but not something they would be comfortable with on a regular basis. The participation, response, or emotionalism can be too much for them. In addition, if whites walk away from church and they've not learned something to stimulate their minds, then church was simply a nice experience. The value of the sermon is evaluated by its organization, information, and insights drawn from the text. I'm sure you can see the great divide between the styles of many white and black churches.

I believe that both preaching and teaching, both informing and inspiring, are critical for the multicultural church to meet the needs of its congregants. The best of both worlds is what God intended anyway. Can you imagine a church that is only academic? How limiting would that be? Can you imagine a church that is only action oriented? God desires for his church to learn and to live his Word. He desires his people to be stimulated intellectually and emotionally. He wants believers to live in stereo, using both their heads and hearts. Groove strategists must adjust the levels of preaching and teaching within the church. They must adjust how often the topic is discussed, the types of people who are elevated to leadership, and the style and content of communication.

MULTICULTURAL MUSIC

If a ministry is going to practice the dance of multicultural ministry, then the rhythms of race will definitely come through in the music. Many professional musicians will argue that there is no such thing as black music, white music, Asian music, and so on. I agree that music shouldn't be classified stereotypically, but ministry leaders need to be aware that many people do associate certain genres with race. A classical piece will be seen as white music, even if it's being played by a black woman. And if a white man is rapping the lyrics of "Amazing Grace," it will be heard as black style.

However, because North American culture is becoming more multicultural, it is becoming less common for people to make these associations. On a typical day in a Maryland suburb, one can drive up to a stop light and hear (or should I say feel) the subwoofer of the car playing rap in the next lane. One used to assume the driver is a black kid. Not anymore. That guy in baggy pants and a baseball cap turned sideways might be as white as Billy Graham. (If it's an old Asian woman with shades bopping her head to the beat, we'll all know that this crossover race thing has gone a bit too far!)

Bridgeway's music ministry serves up its music much like a meal for guests. Often when people invite others for dinner, they will serve a meal that is safe. You hope to deliver a dish to the table that will be, if not delectable, at least palatable. Unless you've invited guests who prefer specific ethnic foods, it is wise to go with something that most people will enjoy.

The same is true for music in a multicultural church. Every multicultural body must find its own mainstream dish. It may be hymns with a little spice, or worship choruses with hymns blended in. It may be traditional hymns arranged in a white, black, African, or Latino style. It just depends on the talent God has brought to your church. At our church, we have written over 130 worship songs that define our multicultural main course.

In addition to the main course, side dishes can really make or break the taste of a meal. Because my wife is Korean, she loves kimchee. Kimchee is a spicy pickled cabbage that will blow the head off of the average pasta lover. When we invite non-Korean guests to the

Andersons for dinner, we provide various Korean side dishes for our guests to experience. Some items they enjoy; some not. But the side dishes are an opportunity for them to discover foods they would have otherwise never known existed.

At Bridgeway, we use ethnic and extreme (relatively speaking) forms of music as side dishes to the mainstream worship. Attenders at our church will have the opportunity to taste rap, rock, classical, jazz, and yes, sometimes even country. These side dishes may come in the form of a solo, a duet, a chorale ensemble, a gospel choir, dance, rap, hip hop, or a screaming guitar piece. Being exposed to the side dishes allows guests to have new experiences without discounting the entire meal.

To expect a large number of whites to prefer an entire service of black gospel every week is unrealistic. To expect a large number of blacks to enjoy eighteenth-century hymns accompanied by a pipe organ would be a stretch. A church that has settled on one style of specialized or ethnic music as their mainstream is probably unicultural, not multicultural. Even if the church is multicolored, it may still be classified in style and substance as a white church or a black church. Multiple colors of skin within a church do not a multicultural church make! A vibrant multicultural church allows multiple cultures freedom of expression through a variety of art forms.

In my view, there are too many churches that serve meat and forget about the vegetarians, and too many churches that focus on the vegetarians and leave out the meat-eaters. A multicultural church serves up a musical meal that seeks to include every group. In the next chapter, I will explain the concept of inclusion as it relates to multicultural church ministry and race.

chapter ten

GRACISM

EVERY VOLUNTEER WORKER, STAFF MEMBER, CHURCH leader, and pastor needs to learn an important art: the art of experiencing God even when you are exhausted doing ministry. Too often in ministry we're reduced to practicing the lowest of art forms—survival! We're much like a marathon runner who is in the last miles of her run. The arms dangle. The legs wobble. The lungs wheeze. The mind is on autopilot, driving the body to the finish line ever so pathetically. "The spirit is willing, but the flesh is weak." Not another phone call, we say. Not another e-mail, we hope. Not another conflict, we fear. Not another confrontation, we pray. But like the marathon, the race of ministry goes on and on.

It is difficult enough to dance through personality clashes, spiritually immature behaviors, and everyday ministry negotiations. But can you imagine throwing the incendiary ingredient of race relations into the mix of ministry? Something is liable to blow up.

CHURCH EXPLOSIONS

Imagine your church has three pastors reporting to the senior pastor or church board. One is African-American, one is Caucasian, and the other is Latino. It's time for a performance review. This year the Latino pastor has consistently underperformed. However, he really has been the key to the church's entrance into the Latino community. Hiring this pastor has satisfied the Latino community and has led to great evangelistic opportunities. Yet his administrative performance has not met expectations. What should be done? Consultants might advise terminating this staff member for consistent underperformance. Wouldn't that be a mark of good proactive leadership?

Or consider another scenario that actually happened in my church. The creative arts ministry is responsible for creating and using music and other forms of creative art to move the congregation to third base before I come up to bat with my sermon. They operate out of our core values, one of which is to reflect the diversity within our church. One Sunday morning I arrived at the auditorium a few minutes early to discover that the vocal team and the worship leader were all black. The announcements were supposed to be done in a soulful ("black") style. In addition, the speaker for the week was black. (Me!) True, the band was white with one Filipino, and the person doing our announcements was white, but I immediately saw an obvious racial imbalance.

When I asked about it, I was met with a bit of frustration from those involved, which was understandable. A lot of hard work had gone into the development of this service, and now here was the senior pastor questioning strategy shortly before the doors were to open. Apparently a couple of our nonblack vocalists could not fulfill their obligation this week, so replacements had to be found. However, the two replacements were both the "wrong" color for that morning.

The service was to begin in a few moments. What action would you advise a leader to take in those circumstances? Would you cancel all or some of the vocal team who had arrived very early that morning? Would you go with a straight, nonsoulful form of communicating the announcements? Would you cancel the speaker? (Don't answer that one!)

Here is what I did in those critical moments of tension. You decide whether I handled it properly. Although it would mean starting late, I instructed the creative arts technical team to bring two of our nonblack band members forward to stand with the vocal team. This meant resetting monitors, lights, and electrical wires, and rearranging plants and other equipment. Another adjustment I made was to have one of my Caucasian pastors join me on stage to perform the scheduled baby dedications. We are to be ready in season and out, right? I had to inform my associate pastor that his season had come! These adjustments provided the face of diversity necessary to underscore our core values of racial reconciliation and diversity. Any other face would have contradicted the values we've worked so hard to inculcate. During our debriefing forty-eight hours later, the team discussed how this faux pas had happened and how to insure that it does not reoccur.

DEFINING GRACISM

This scenario was a lesson in what I call *gracism*. I define racism as speaking, acting, or thinking negatively about someone based solely on his or her race. A common definition of grace is the unmerited favor of God. Extending such favor and kindness to others is how we, as Christ-followers, demonstrate this grace practically from day to day. When one merges the definition of racism, which is negative, with grace, which is positive, a new term emerges—gracism.

Gracism is the positive extension of favor toward others based on race. Such favor is not biblically unmerited. The apostle Paul encouraged the Galatians to do good to all people as they had the opportunity, but especially to those who belong to the family of believers (Gal. 6:10). The positive extension of favor toward certain people is not favoritism, which James warns against (James 2:9). James was writing in the context of loving all people and not discriminating against the poor. To discriminate, exclude, and not love everyone is sin. Notice that James's comments about favoritism in 2:9 follow the command to love your neighbor in 2:8. His point is that we are to love everyone and not discriminate against anyone. Does this mean that extending favor in an environment where everyone is loved and treated with equal respect is wrong? I say no. Like Paul said, we must do good to all people. James appeals to us to love all people and discriminate against none. This does not preclude extending favor to specific groups. God has done this throughout the ages. A cursory reading of the Scriptures regarding widows, orphans, and the poor would underscore the point. It is possible to extend favor and still be fair.

Distinct from favoritism, whereby one grants favor because of elitism, ethnic superiority, or commonality, gracism reaches outside these boxes. A *gracist* reaches across ethnic lines and across racial borders to lend specific assistance and extra grace to those who are different, on the fringe, or marginalized. This person or group can be of any color, culture, or gender.

Gracism, unlike racism, doesn't focus on race for negative purposes such as discrimination. Gracism focuses on race for the positive purposes of ministry and service. When the grace of God is communicated through the beauty of race, then you have gracism. It is not always easy to lift up the values of diversity and inclusion while balancing other values such as excellence in a Sunday morning service or employee performance. However, evaluating the tradeoffs is critical. For example, is a Sunday service really excellent if everything is executed well by a unicultural slate of performers? My answer is no. Excellence is when your service, your ministry, and your leadership activities are executed well by an array of servants who represent the richness of the body of Christ.

At Bridgeway we have canceled service elements, rearranged stage designs, accommodated staff positions, and brought on team members with an eye toward color and culture. Yes, you can call us gracists!

A gracist recognizes the beauty of diversity. A gracist will go to any length and work as diligently as possible to insure that such beauty is seen and celebrated. Gracists refuse to settle for unicultural segregation without doing all he or she can to include diversity at all levels of the church.

In a perfect world, such work would not be necessary. But in a racialized society, gracism is necessary. Just as sin causes humankind to be in need of God's grace, the radical inclusion of races within our churches is paramount if the church is going to overcome the historically devastating effects of racism. Gracism must be extended intentionally, but without confusing intentionality with ramrodding race quotas down the throats of church members. Delicate leadership will influence others to see race relations as one of the ultimate expressions of grace-giving and grace-living.

Giving an Extra Measure of Grace to a Staff Member

Earlier I mentioned the fictitious case of an underperforming pastor. I actually know a pastor who was emotionally exhausted by having to terminate a staff member who was of a different color and culture. Dealing with the performance issues had much to do with the staff member's cultural background. Understanding this, and knowing that the loss of this staff member would have negative effects on the church, the pastor gave extra grace and worked much longer to keep this staff member on board for as long as he could. But other issues made the termination necessary. As I consulted with the supervising pastor throughout the process, it was evident that multicultural ministry requires an extra measure of grace because of race. The supervising pastor was struggling to be a good leader and gracist at the same time, a balance that many churches do not have the privilege of weighing. Unlike God, we do not have an unlimited supply of grace, nor are we to take advantage of the grace that God so generously offers. The time came when the pastor had to terminate the staff member, lest he enable long term underperformance.

Gracism affects not only the performance of employees and the structure of Sunday morning staging but also hiring practices. Often the term affirmative action elicits an array of responses. When it comes to multicultural ministry, not only is staging important but staffing is essential. Whether one calls it affirmative action, employment equity, or something else, the bottom line is that if you want to become or sustain a significant multicultural ministry, the leadership and servanthood ranks of the church must be multicultural as well.

The Grace of a Unique Staff Arrangement

Venus Santiago-Glass affectionately refers to herself as a Puerto Rican girl from the Bronx. She was divorced when she started attending Bridgeway Community Church. Then Venus got saved. As she grew in her faith she began to realize that her current dating situation was not built on a godly foundation, so she said goodbye to her boyfriend. God began to impress on Venus her need to develop spiritually in several areas, one of which was her materialistic heart. This very talented woman, who had nearly three hundred employees reporting to her, was vice president in a corporation where she had been climbing the ladder of success with great determination.

Meanwhile, I sensed that when Bridgeway reached five or six hundred, it was going to need an operations manager to run the daily operations. (I am deficient in that area.) The elders agreed and we budgeted for the hire. I was committed not to hire another black or white staffer; if we were going to evolve into a truly multicultural church, we could not settle for a biracial staff. I prayed for applicants. I networked for applicants. I searched the country for applicants. Although we had people apply, I was unsuccessful in finding the right racial fit coupled with the skills and passion that would enable multicultural success.

Two years later the church had grown to about seven hundred and fifty attenders and I had no operations manager. Yikes! Now I was getting desperate. Then God used a couple of people in our church to put forward Venus's name. Of course, this corporate VP wasn't about to give up her six-figure job to run a church staff of ten or so, or would she? Venus prayed about it and contemplated the position for several months. Finally she agreed. Within one year we had restructured to accommodate our growth and all was going extremely well. Then God decided to really throw a monkey wrench into our system.

Venus announced good and bad news. The good news was that she was getting married. Hooray! The bad news was that she was moving to Florida. Ouch!

We all agreed that Venus' marriage was right. The man that Venus was going to marry was Reggie, her first husband. It was a story of God's grace and reconciliation power. But I just couldn't believe that she would no longer be working with me and the church. We all loved her. We all watched her grow spiritually. We all witnessed her incredible gift of managerial leadership. I suggested that we simply pray for a few months about this.

After a few months of prayer, the Lord laid on my heart an unusual way to keep Venus in our ministry. I asked Venus if we could keep her as an employee part-time and have her commute from Florida. Amazingly, she said she and Reggie had been thinking the same thing independent of each other. After floating this unconventional idea to the pastors and elders, we agreed on a plan. We would hire a business manager who would work full-time in our office and report to Venus. Every month Venus would fly up to Maryland so that she could have regular meetings, stage time in our services, and social connection with the people she works with.

Although many businesses are used to this kind of arrangement, it was a new thing for us. But why was I so adamant about not losing Venus? Why was I so willing to hold out instead of hiring someone who didn't fit the profile of our core values? Was it favoritism? No. Was it discrimination? No. Was it affirmative action? You answer that! Beyond Venus's impeccable skills, godly heart, and professionalism was something that inspired me to go the extra mile to keep her on my team. There is one word that explains what made me stretch further, work harder, wait longer, pray steadier, and search deeper for an innovative solution. Gracism!

Grace and Reconciliation Live

I was offered a wonderful opportunity to host a live radio talk show for two hours on Sunday evenings. The show would be about building bridges of reconciliation. As far as we knew, this was the first show on Christian radio in which the entire program would be centered on reconciliation. And we were going to do it right in the nation's capital. Wow, I was very excited. After making a pitch to tag-team the program with a cohost, I accepted the opportunity. The next task was to choose my cohost. I knew that if the show was going to be about racial reconciliation and about building bridges across many other divides, my counterpart could not be black. Within hours I had chosen Tracey, a Caucasian female who served in our music and creative arts ministry. Tracey has a wonderful voice and a beautiful spirit. Together we would tag-team this groundbreaking talk show where people call in live to ask me any question they want about race relations or multicultural issues. Tracey was not an affirmative-action choice but a gracist choice. She was skilled, qualified, and talented, but in addition, she represented those who were not like me and would be an asset to the bridge-building process through the airwaves. Gracism indeed.

DON'T BECOME COLOR-BLIND

Dealing with race can add an extra dimension of stress to the already exhausting work of ministry. But the richness of doing life within a blended body of believers far outweighs the stress. Struggling with race may be like struggling to finish a race. Remember that marathoner with the dangling arms, wobbly legs, and wheezing lungs? No matter how stressful the race, she will receive something that many never will. She will have the thrill of crossing the finish line. If you or I could catch her once she fell into the tape at the end of the race and could ask her if the training, conditioning, dreaming, dieting, and even doubting were worth that moment, she would say, "Yes, yes, a hundred times, yes!"

When gracism flows freely within a church, life and ministry may not always be easy, but you will testify that the wholeness of community that comes with multicultural unity is worth it. You will be willing to work even harder to stage a service of excellence or go the extra mile for an employee. When asked if it is worth it, I'm sure you will say, "Yes, yes, a hundred times, yes!"

My prayer is that the church, whether Anglo, African, or Afghan, would refuse to be color-blind. Why would we ever want to dull a sense that we've been given by our creator? We don't need color-blind stages, staffs, and structures. We need churches who know how to see beauty and celebrate diversity. Who among us would ever desire to walk through a garden to behold only one color and one kind of flower?

I enjoy roses, but not just red ones. I enjoy white, yellow, and pink roses too. When you mix a few of these roses with purple and yellow irises, carnations, and lilies, along with a little greenery wrapped together with a bow, you have a beautiful bouquet. When God sees his children, he appreciates their unique colors and categories. But when he gathers them all together in his divine palm, he is holding a masterful bouquet. God is the ultimate gracist.

The divine gardener is coming back to pick out his masterful bouquet of children from his earthly garden. He is coming back for one bouquet, one bride, one body. He's coming back for one church with many congregations. God's grace flows to one race, the human race. Those of us from every tribe and language and people and nation who are recipients of grace have the awesome joy of calling each other brothers and sisters because we all have the same heavenly father. Yes, I am your brother from another mother, but thank God we both have the same daddy! Like the effect that brilliantly colored leaves falling from a New England tree in autumn have on the average human being, I wonder if the diversity of God's children falling at his feet in worship simply takes his breath away.

@

In the next section we will see how the Lord of the dance has organized the rhythms of grace through biblical history until eternity.

part 4

THE LORD OF THE DANCE

chapter eleven

BROKEN RECORD

DO YOU REMEMBER EIGHT-TRACK TAPES? HOW ABOUT records? If you still play vinyl records on a turntable, I hate to tell you this but you are old. Record albums and eight tracks were once the rage in music technology. Now you're lucky if you can get a cassette tape player (*if* you want one) in your next new vehicle. In this day and age one can play music from the Internet with just a computer and phone line. Times have changed.

Before they were five, my children were incorporating into their everyday language terms like CD, DVD, VCR, VHS, AOL, PC, dot-com, CD-ROM, and mouse (not the kind that eats cheese). It would not be unusual for one of my children to say something like this: "Dad, while I was on the PC I read that we can rent a DVD from AOL since our VHS is still stuck in the VCR. And by the way, Dad, it's my turn to choose the CD that we listen to in the SUV on our way to BK [Burger King] for dinner tonight!" If I am to respond in code to my kids, I suppose the only thing they would want from me is "OK !"

While language and technology have changed from generation to generation, the desire for good music has not. The same is true of the Word of God. "The grass withers and the flowers fall, but the word of the Lord stands forever" (1 Peter 1:24–25). While preachers, theologians, and Bible teachers have not always communicated the Word of God clearly, I believe that the church of Jesus Christ has been enlightened over the past generation to declare what the Bible has to say regarding racial unity. This hasn't always been the case. The eight-track theology of racial superiority taught in some theological circles even as late as the 1970s and '80s to justify American slavery was obsolete, incompatible with "biblical technology." Although many people once held to misinterpretations of the Bible, the broken record of racial superiority is still played by only a few unenlightened collectors.

Allow me to guide you through what I call the Divine-Human Timeline. It is a survey of fourteen biblical categories that will give you a bird's-eye perspective of race. I must warn you that the timeline is didactic. If you will stick with me, though, you will see how the Bible ties together theologically as one story. By viewing the Old and New Testaments from a broad perspective, you will discover the heart of God as it relates to oneness.

THE DIVINE-HUMAN TIMELINE
Creation (Gen. 1 – 2)

In the first sentence of the first verse of the first chapter in the Bible, we see the oneness of God. "In the beginning God," we read in Genesis 1:1. In this verse the word used for God is *Elohim*, which in the Hebrew language has a plural ending. This indicates union within the Godhead. God the Father, God the Son, and God the Holy Spirit created the heavens and the earth. There is oneness and unity in the triune God. Genesis 1:26 ("Let us make people in our image, to be like ourselves . . ." [NLT]) uses the plural pronouns *us* and *our* to indicate yet again the triune God.

Not only was there a sense of unity in the Godhead but there was unity in creation. After God created everything, he said that it was good. When God completed the crown of creation, humankind, he saw all that he had made and stated that it was very good.

Communion (Gen. 2)

In the Garden of Eden oneness and communion existed between God and humankind. Can you imagine oneness and fellowship with God without the barriers of sin, shame, or a need for confession of sin? Once Eve was created, she experienced oneness with Adam.

THE DIVINE-HUMAN TIMELINE
A Biblical Rationale for Multicultural Ministry

Period	Scripture	Key Event	Theme	Details
CREATION	Gen. 1-2			
COMMUNION	Gen. 2			
CONTROL/CURSE	Gen. 3	The Fall	Struggle between submission and dominance	Between: • Satan & God • Satan & humankind • People & God • People & People
CONTENTION	Gen. 4		Struggle for self-worth	• One upmanship • "I'm better than you mentality."
CATASTROPHE	Gen. 6		Struggle for survival	• Violence: survival from each other • Destruction: survival from the elements • Judgment: survival from God's judgment
COVENANT WITH NOAH	Gen. 9:9		Safety found in God	
CURSE	Gen. 9:18-10:32		Slavery based on race theologically justified	• Curse of Ham was the misguided theological basis for slavery in America & is still taught in some seminaries • Most evangelical seminaries rejected this teaching by the 1970s
CONFUSION	Gen. 11		Separation of languages & cultures by God	• Divine segregation
COVENANT WITH ABRAHAM	Gen. 12		Selected remnant by God	• Divine covenant • God hand-picked a remnant
CAPTIVITY	Exodus		Salvation from slavery & captivity	• Divine deliverance
CHRIST	The Gospels	The Cross	Sacrifice for all humankind including Jews & Gentiles	• Divine sacrifice
NEW CREATION/COMMUNION OF THE COMING OF CHRIST	Acts 2	The Church		• Divine integration
CONSUMMATION OF THE AGE INTO ETERNITY	Revelation	The Rapture		

Israel · The Church Age

They were naked and unashamed (Gen. 2:25). They freely related without division and conflict. In creation we recognize oneness between God and people; oneness between man and woman; and oneness within all of creation on the earth. The environment was not cursed and animals were not killed. There was a great sense of unity in the Garden of Eden; no death, no division, no domination or superiority. It was a time of communion.

Control/Curse (Gen. 3)

Before the fall into sin Adam didn't have a problem relating to God, his wife, or his work. God told Adam to take care of the earth. Adam was capable of completing the mission God had given him once God blessed him with a mate at his side (and from his side). But when Satan, in the form of a serpent, tempted Eve to eat the fruit of the forbidden tree, a struggle for control ensued.

Lucifer had been seeking to overturn God's power even before God evicted him from heaven. Eve now struggled to choose between what God commanded her to avoid and the desire of her will. Since the Garden of Eden, the struggle to determine who's in charge continues.

After the fall, when Adam and Eve disobeyed God's command not to eat from the tree in the center of the Garden, everything was negatively affected, including worship and work. Fellowship and unity between God and Adam and Eve were broken. As God walked through the cool of the Garden, Adam and Eve hid, trying to cover their shame with fig leaves. Once God confronted Adam, he of course blamed his wife. (Some things never change!) Eve also passed the buck of blame to the serpent.

As a result of their sin, God allowed the consequences of death to affect the land and all relationships. From this point in Genesis until the book of Revelation, we can see two story lines. One is the unfolding of sin's consequences on the human condition. The parallel story is the unfolding of God's plan of redemption through Jesus Christ to deliver us from eternal consequences.

Contention (Gen. 4)

As the story of sin's consequences unfolds, we see the spiral of depravity leading to violence, murder, war, polygamy, and more. It was as if a perfect score of music degenerated into a screeching and horrid sound of dissonance. Yet the story of redemption is the story of God's taking his out-of-tune creation and recreating a new sound of oneness in Christ. God is taking us back to that place where his creation dances freely in fellowship with him and each other. God is preparing a new heaven and a new earth for his people, where we will once again have perfect worship, work, and oneness with God and one another. But the day of our singing as one chorus from one sheet of music cannot be found in biblical history.

By the time we get to Genesis 4 humankind is singing the blues as the communion of Genesis 1 and 2 is supplanted by contention among brothers. Oneness in worship has been exchanged for competition. Cain compared his sacrifice to God with the sacrifice of his brother, Abel, and felt inferior. Even after God warned Cain not to allow sin to master him, Cain killed his brother in cold blood out of jealousy. It was the ultimate expression of one-upmanship, of the I-am-better-than-you mentality.

This wasn't the first time the sounds of death had been heard on the earth. Do you remember what God did when he found Adam and Eve in the Garden of Eden after they sinned? Genesis 3:21 says, "The LORD God made garments of skin for Adam and his wife and clothed them." Please don't miss how profound this concept of redemption is as God performs this act of mercy. God killed one of his animals and ripped off its skin to cover his children's shame. The sound of death echoed throughout the Garden and in the ears of animals and humans for the first time. Yet it was God's will to shed the blood of an innocent third party to cover the shame of Adam and Eve.

Is this not a vivid picture of Jesus Christ, who would one day be the ultimate third party, shedding his innocent blood to cover humankind and cleanse them from sin and shame? Fig leaves could not cover the shame of humanity, and the sacrifices of animals didn't have the power to cleanse humans from their sin. Only through the shed blood of Christ do we have the remission for our sins. The unfolding plan of redemption parallels the unfolding consequences of sin's effect on the human condition. What the Garden heard on that day was the sound of redemption.

As a result of sin, Cain murdered his brother, Abel. God confronted and banished Cain from his presence and people. Absurdly, many people have misinterpreted the meaning of this banishment. Maybe you've heard of this misconception. In Genesis 4:15 it is recorded that God put a mark on Cain so that he would not be killed if he was identified as a wanderer in the wilderness. Many people have interpreted this mark as a sign of evil as opposed to a sign of God's mercy. Simply put, some have suggested that God put the "mark of Cain" on black people, that Cain's banishment was the banishment of black people to Africa. Just one of the theological myths of race.

Catastrophe (Gen. 6)

Because of the violence and evil of humankind, God was sorry that he had ever created humans, and his heart was filled with pain (Gen. 6:6). God chose to wipe out every life form he had created, save Noah, his family, and a pair of animals from each species. The judgment of God came through a flood.

Covenant with Noah (Gen. 9:9 – 16)

After the world was flooded, Noah and his family were saved and given the task of repopulating the earth. God promised not to destroy the earth by water again and made the rainbow a sign of his promise.

Have you ever stopped to look at the beauty of the colors in a rainbow? Shouldn't the church of Jesus Christ be a human rainbow so uniquely beautiful that it causes people to stop and marvel? Unfortunately, in many cases, that's not what happens.

Curse (Gen. 9 – 10)

Another passage of the Bible that has been misinterpreted is the "curse of Ham." After the flood, Noah drank too much, fell asleep naked, and was found by his sons. Ham saw his father's nakedness while his two brothers covered up his "shame." Genesis 9:24–25 says, "When Noah awoke from his wine and found out what his youngest son had done to him, he said, 'Cursed be Canaan! The lowest of slaves will he be to his brothers.'"

Because Canaan was one of Ham's four sons, some theologians interpreted the curse to be directed to Ham and all of his descendants. However, the curse was not on Ham directly but on Canaan, his son. The reason why it is important to establish who the curse was on is because Ham is the father of black people. He represents people of color. Canaan was obviously the bearer of this curse, and the Bible records that the Canaanites were continually subjugated by Israel (Josh. 9:23; 1 Kings 9:20–21).

For years the theological misinterpretation of Noah's curse and the myth of black inferiority was used to justify slavery in America. Slavery was a heinous crime against humanity. African people were kidnapped from their homeland, sold, sometimes even by their own people, shipped across the sea, and separated from their families. Whippings, beatings, burnings, brandings, rapes, castrations, torture, and hangings were par for the course.

Generations of slavery, segregation, and civil rights battles have left the African-American community clamoring for identity. They live on the hyphen between the words African and

American. They live in that hyphenated place between American culture and African roots, trying to find some sense of identity being American yet holding onto the African heritage that was ripped from their souls and psyche. I am American and also of African descent. I don't want to live in Africa because it is not my culture or home. Yet I derive great dignity from my African heritage.

Italian-Americans have a country to tie their heritage to, namely, Italy. Korean-Americans have Korea with which they identify. German-Americans connect their lineage to Germany, and so on. But can any of us identify a place called Black? Of course not. For generations, black people from Africa were forbidden to identify their countries of origin, their language, or their cultural roots. Stripped of culture, they were not given rights or citizenship as Americans, nor were they allowed to identify with their countries in Africa. So what were they? What are they? Africans? No and yes. Americans? No and yes. Property of Americans? No longer, and thankfully, never again.

It is natural to want to seek one's roots. Some of you may remember Alex Haley's book *Roots*, which was made into a television movie. (I think every American, regardless of color, should watch a video or DVD of *Roots*. Most public libraries will have a copy. In my opinion, it is one of the best dramatic educational experiences of the emotional history of blacks in America.) I am who I am because of my roots. There has been much interest by blacks to get in touch with their African roots through music, apparel, art, education, and other means. I never criticize those who want to go back to their history, because often therein lies the musical score for their identity and destiny.

Thankfully, in modern times the overwhelming majority of Bible scholars and seminaries have overturned the erroneous theological arguments that used to be put forth to support the idea of black inferiority and to justify slavery. The mark of Cain and the curse of Ham

have been handily debunked![1] I think we can all agree that racism is
not a skin problem but a sin problem.

Confusion (Gen. 11)

We now move on to Genesis 11. The whole world had one language. The people of the day decided to build a tower to the heavens to glorify themselves. God was not happy with this. His creatures
were worshiping themselves and creation, not the Creator. So God
confused their language until they could not understand each other
and then scattered them over all the earth. (The word *babel* means
"confused.") It is from this point in biblical history that we see what
I call divine segregation.

Covenant with Abraham (Gen. 12)

Now, instead of working with a scattered population of people,
God chose to make a divine covenant with one people group, the
Israelites. In Genesis 12:2–3, God made a divine covenant with
Abram, saying, "I will make you into a great nation and I will bless
you; I will make your name great, and you will be a blessing. I will
bless those who bless you, and whoever curses you I will curse; and
all peoples on earth will be blessed through you." God worked with
and through the Hebrew people throughout the rest of history as a
sign of his redemption. Through the descendents of Abram, or Abra-
ham, God would send the messiah to redeem the world to the Jew
first, then to the Gentile (Rom. 1:16). God handpicked the Jewish
people as a remnant of his grace.

Captivity (Exodus)

The Hebrew people were enslaved in horrific captivity by the
Egyptians. God called his servant Moses to go back to Egypt, a place

---

[1]See, for example, John H. Walton, *Genesis*, The NIV Application Commentary
Series (Grand Rapids: Zondervan, 2001), 355–56.

where he once was heralded as great, to set them free and lead them to the Promised Land. Through the acts and miraculous signs of God through Moses, we witness divine deliverance from slavery and captivity.

From the point of their journey out of Egypt to the Promised Land until the day of Christ, the Jewish people experienced a tumultuous relationship with God as recorded through the prophets, kings, and wisdom literature of the Old Testament.

Christ (the Gospels)

Jesus' life, death, burial, and resurrection were for the sole purpose of redeeming humankind. He reversed the curse of sin and death that came through the first Adam by crushing Satan's head, as promised in Genesis 3:15: "And I will put enmity between you and the woman, and between your offspring and hers; he will crush your head, and you will strike his heel." In this verse, God was referring to Jesus as the head-crusher of the devil, thus nullifying the sting of death and the victory of the grave (1 Cor. 15:55–57).

The divine sacrifice of God was to forsake his son on the cross. Christ's death was equivalent to the eternity that humans would experience if they were separated from and forsaken by God forever. Jesus was the innocent third party who covered us and cleansed us from our sin and shame. Once a person believes by faith that Christ is their substitute for the eternal capital punishment they must bear as a penalty for their sin, they can receive God's power by faith.

Jesus, the savior, was establishing his new kingdom when he drafted his disciples and sent them out as apostles to lay the foundation of the Christian church, which would be infused by the power of the Holy Spirit. Do you remember the first two categories in our timeline, Creation (Gen. 1) and Communion (Gen. 2)? As the second Adam, Jesus through his work on the cross reestablished a new creation and a new communion through new believers on the earth. As a result, Christians experience restored worship, work, and oneness. The unfolding plan of redemption began in Genesis 3 and continued through the Old Testament sacrificial system to the cross, where Jesus performed the ultimate act of sacrifice and love. Jesus Christ is our only way to God the Father.

New Creation/Communion (Acts 2)

After his resurrection, Jesus appeared to many. In the Upper Room, as noted in Acts 1, Jesus spoke to his disciples for the final time before ascending to heaven. Jesus explained that the Holy Spirit would come with power and enable the disciples to be witnesses throughout the world (v. 8). In the second chapter of Acts, the Holy Spirit descended with power, inaugurating the New Testament church. Because of Christ's work on the cross and because of the power of the Holy Spirit in believers, you and I can experience God-honoring worship and work, and oneness with God and other believers.

The reason why believers experience new communion with one another is because of something I refer to as divine integration. In Acts 2, while the apostles were praying, the Holy Spirit suddenly fell on the people in the Upper Room and they began to speak in tongues, or previously unlearned and unknown languages. While thousands were in Jerusalem for the holy day of Pentecost, the Spirit's movement on the Upper Room caused such a party that bystanders assumed the participants were drunk with wine. Yet they were bewildered because they could hear the gospel being preached in their native languages.

Contrast these events with those in Genesis 11, where we learned of the divine segregation of God. Humankind, speaking one language, schemed to build a self-glorifying tower. God scattered everyone around the world, giving them different languages. In Acts 2

God brings everyone back together again, but this time under the
power of the Holy Spirit. Although there were over a dozen people
groups present at Pentecost, who spoke different languages, the text
tells us that in the streets of Jerusalem on that day, they were all
"declaring the wonders of God" (Acts 2:11). The declaration of the
wonders of God is the one language of all believers, regardless of
dialect or tongue.

True unity is found only in God. Worship of God (as opposed
to worshiping humanity or creation) is the language of all believers.
While it is true that unbelievers desire peace, seek diversity, and
want unity, the truth is that only within the body of Christ can ultimate communion and racial unity occur. Sensitivity, civility, and tolerance are critical for a diverse world, but true unity, love,
acceptance, and oneness come only through the worship of the
Creator, who causes us to be united by the Spirit. Those who worship God the Father must do so in Spirit and in truth (John 4:24).
At Pentecost people from all over the world were unified not
because of a holy day or the building of a tower. They were unified
because of the Holy One, who was building for himself one household of praise (Eph. 2:19–22).

Coming of Christ Again (New Testament)

The rest of the New Testament, from Romans to the third chapter of Revelation, is about God's people worshiping, working, and
being together as one purified bride preparing for her husband. The
church of Jesus Christ is to anticipate the return of Christ. Believers in Christ will be raptured and escorted into the consummation
of the age.

Consummation of the Age into Eternity (Revelation)

When God escorts his people into the eternal state, according
to Revelation 21:1–4, he will have created a new heaven and a new

earth. The old heaven and earth will be destroyed, and we will return to the worship, work, and oneness of the Garden of Eden. Such union with God and creation is a vision that connects the end of the Bible to its beginning, where God said all things were "very good" (Gen. 1:31). Yet in the new heaven and earth there will be a multitude of grace-recipients from every tribe, language, people, and tongue who fall down at the feet of their savior to worship the worthy Lamb who took away the sins of the world, Jesus Christ (Gen. 4–7).

THE LORD OF THE DANCE

To summarize, God created the heavens and the earth, where great worship, work, and oneness existed. The music of creation and the dance of communion between God and humankind was divine. The consequences of sin led to the curse of death and brokenness, which degenerated into contention, catastrophe, and confusion. As a result of his mercy, God chose to establish a covenant with the Israelites. God, in keeping his covenant with the people, delivered the Israelites from captivity. God's people continued to rebel and reject him throughout their history, though often they longed for a messiah to deliver them once and for all. God sent Christ, the anointed messiah, to begin the work of a new creation as he completed his redemptive plan through his death, burial, and resurrection. Those in the body of Christ are new creations who experience new communion from every tribe, nation, people, and language. We have the power and calling to dance together as we worship the Lord in Spirit and in truth until the coming of Christ and the consummation of the age. One day you and I will be in the perfect place of worship, work, and oneness again. The broken record of division will never be played again! That's the story of the Bible.

Can you see that the whole of Scripture is about oneness? God himself is one. Man and woman are married to become one. Those of us in the family of God are called to be one body. Jesus' longest recorded prayer is that we would experience oneness (John 17). The plan of redemption is all about bringing humans back into oneness with God.

When I explain this didactic lesson in seminars, the scholarly types in the group get excited about the connections that surface. However, the greatest emotion usually comes from those who realize (many for the first time) that the idea of reconciliation is a biblical one.

I'll never forget a man named Earl, who was elated after I taught this material at a roundtable luncheon for leaders on the East Coast. Earl leaned forward in the meeting and said, "My church needs to hear this! How can we talk about diversity and racial reconciliation without seeing how biblically rooted it is? Wow, I can't believe all of this is in the Bible!" I was thrilled because the social interest that motivated him to attend the luncheon transformed into a biblical conviction because of the renewing of his mind.

In the meantime, let's do our best as a multicultural army of believers to win others to Christ through multicultural evangelism. I will explain these rhythms in the next chapter.

chapter twelve

RHYTHMS OF MULTICULTURAL EVANGELISM

THE EVANGELICAL CHURCH HAS DEVELOPED MANY methods of evangelism over time. Perhaps you've been part of some of the recent ones: Evangelism Explosion, lifestyle evangelism, and the seeker movement are a few. Yet for all the various methods and perspectives, modern evangelicalism has been resoundingly silent when it comes to multicultural evangelism, relegating cross-cultural evangelism to behind-the-scenes discussions in the missions departments of Bible colleges, seminaries, and churches. Yet isn't thinking through evangelism as it relates to race in North America germane to outreach?

I remember having a frank conversation with my friend, Lee Strobel. He had written an evangelism book called *Inside the Mind of Unchurched Harry and Mary.* Shortly after the book came out, I sat with Lee in his office. "What about unchurched Leroy and Latifah, or unchurched Manuel and Maria?" I asked. Lee looked at me and said honestly, "David, we [meaning him and those in leadership at the predominantly Caucasian church he was in] don't really know how to reach Latifah or Manuel. We're hoping that you will teach us through your example."

Lee's candid statement inspired me because it validated my vision for multicultural ministry as a young pastor. On the other hand, his words were reflective of how insular the church had become in the United States. That's not the way it's supposed to be.

Multicultural evangelism is sharing the gospel message with someone from a racial or ethnic background different from your own.

Several passages in the New Testament show an inextricable link between evangelism and multicultural ministry. Let's take a look at a few of them.

THE GREAT MULTIETHNIC COMMISSION (MATT. 28:18–20)

Commonly referred to as the Great Commission, this passage in Matthew records Jesus' command to his disciples to make disciples of every nation. The command was in three parts: going, baptizing, and teaching.

"Therefore go and make disciples of all nations, baptizing them in the name of the Father and of the Son and of the Holy Spirit, and teaching them to obey everything I have commanded you. And surely I am with you always, to the very end of the age" (Matt. 28:19–20).

The phrase "make disciples" satisfied the question of what Jesus' followers were commissioned to do. But the phrase "of all nations" specified the extensive target Jesus had in mind. The Greek term translated here as "nation" is *ethnos*. In other words, Jesus was commanding his followers to make disciples of people from all ethnic backgrounds. There was no longer a chosen people for whom God reserved the gospel message. Matthew Henry, English nonconformist minister and Bible commentator, said that the covenant of peculiarity made with the Jewish people was cancelled by this time.[1] All nations, all peoples, all languages, all cultures, and all ethnic groups were to be evangelized, in contrast to Matthew 10:5–6, where the apostle's message was restricted just to the people of Israel. The dividing wall between Jew and Gentile was broken by the death, burial, and resurrection of Jesus Christ (Eph. 2:14).

For the disciples to obey the Great Commission, they had to face the inevitability of cross-cultural, multiethnic ministry. At the very

---

[1]Matthew Henry, *Matthew Henry's Commentary on the Whole Bible* (Peabody, Mass.: Hendrickson, 1991), 1775.

start of the first-century church, Peter and the other apostles confronted racial and ethnic challenges head on. Remember the story of
the first deacons? The Hellenistic, Greek-speaking Jews were mur-
muring that their poor widows were not receiving fair distribution
from the wealthy. The Aramaic-speaking Jews, like the apostles themselves, had neglected this minority group. The apostles addressed the
problem by appointing Greek-speaking deacons to serve the widows.
The first church practiced the dance of cross-cultural ministry and
multiethnic evangelism from the outset, because of the Great Multiethnic Commission.

WORLD WIDE WITNESSES (ACTS 1:8)

We find another example of God's intention for multicultural
evangelism just prior to Jesus' ascension. Jesus told his disciples that
they would be his witnesses not only in Jerusalem but also in Judea,
Samaria, and to the uttermost parts of the earth.

The disciples would not be alone in this monumental task. The
Holy Spirit would empower them and the generations of Christians
to follow as they practiced the dance of multicultural ministry. The
disciples were called to evangelize beyond the comfort of their own
ethnic group, reaching out to those who lived in other communities,
cities, and provinces. The Spirit's power did the first work of multicultural evangelism when Peter preached the gospel message to Jews
and other ethnic groups on the streets of Jerusalem at Pentecost (Acts
2). The audience included "Parthians, Medes and Elamites; residents
of Mesopotamia, Judea and Cappadocia, Pontus and Asia, Phrygia
and Pamphylia, Egypt and the parts of Libya near Cyrene; visitors
from Rome (both Jews and converts to Judaism); Cretans and Arabs"
(Acts 2:9–11). Thousands of people from various ethnicities came to
know the Lord Jesus as savior on that day as they danced to a new
rhythm of salvation (Acts 2:41).

Notice that Peter and the apostles ministered to those who came
to their city from various parts of the world. People from scores of

nations have come to North America by foot, rail, automobile, ship, boat, raft, and aircraft. Will your church and mine accept the challenge to minister to them? As our multiethnic evangelism produces multiethnic disciples, will we allow other ethnic peoples to minister with us and to us?

A RHYTHMIC LIFESTYLE (1 COR. 9:20–22)

The apostle Paul spoke of reaching both Jews and non-Jews—that is, Gentiles. In his letter to the Corinthians, the apostle argued that in order for him to win non-Jews, he was willing to reach out to them by foregoing his Jewish customs and embracing Gentile customs. Paul never conformed to other cultures to the point of crossing into sinful behavior, but he conducted himself in such a way that he could identify with the people he was trying to reach. The New Testament attests to the apostle's ability to reach across ethnic lines (Acts 20:21; Eph. 3:6–7).

Paul's outreach went beyond simply announcing the gospel with a deeper level of identification and living cross-culturally for the sake of the gospel (1 Cor. 9:23). Paul adjusted to the rhythm of a different lifestyle in order to reach different people groups. Whenever you and I interact at deeper levels with those from other racial and ethnic backgrounds, our cultural rhythms must adjust. We are challenged to dance to a different beat and sway in a new way.

My wife and I went on a double date to a famous steak house in Baltimore with some friends a short time ago. Above the restaurant was a club lounge with a dance floor surrounded by big leather chairs. As we sat watching the dance floor fill up, it became evident that we were in a Latino-themed club lounge. The music was Latino. The drinks, menu, and art were Latino. But most of all, the dancing was Latino. Everyone was doing the salsa. The salsa has a totally different rhythm than the rhythm my body is used to. And we could see that I wasn't the only one in that situation. We had a good laugh as we witnessed one guy who was clearly dancing to the 1970s disco in his head while everybody else was in the new century.

The point Paul is attempting to convey is that the gospel is about rhythmic living. Learning new-century moves to communicate a timeless message is critical to evangelistic effectiveness. Many churches, and Christians within them, are more committed to keeping disco alive than listening to new sounds and learning new dance rhythms. Had Paul not been willing to conform to different cultures without compromising his convictions, he would have been out of rhythm on the dance floor of multicultural ministry. But because he was willing to dance to a different beat, he propagated the message of Christ on dance floors around the globe.

AMBASSADORS (2 COR. 5:17–21)

The apostle Paul spoke of two things God did for the believer. First, God reconciled the believer to himself (2 Cor. 5:18). As new creations in Christ, believers are reconciled to God and are no longer at enmity with him. God wiped the slate clean and released believers from their sin debt. Second, God has given every believer the ministry of reconciliation. All who are in Christ are ambassadors of Christ (2 Cor. 5:20) called to represent him regardless of ethnic identity. Christians are called to evangelize their world regardless of color, class, or culture.

JESUS' RHYTHMS (JOHN 4:7–43)

In John 4:7–43 we can find a very good example of reconciliation and ambassadorship. A Samaritan woman drawing water from a well encountered Jesus, who reached across ethnic and gender lines to reconcile her to God by asking her for a drink of water. During his conversation with this socially unacceptable woman, Jesus extended the good news of salvation, using water and food as an illustration. In verse 9 the woman clarified the ethic barrier when she said, "You are a Jew and I am a Samaritan woman. How can you ask me for a drink?" Jesus was deliberately building a bridge to cross the ethnic and gender divide. Once this woman understood the good news of salvation, she immediately became an ambassador for Christ. The Samaritan woman returned to her town and shared the good news of Christ with others. As a result, many in the town became followers of Christ (vv. 39–43). Jesus built a bridge to the woman and the woman built a bridge to her community. She was an ambassador of reconciliation after she herself had been reconciled.

Jesus' Rhythm of Intentionality

Notice a few lessons of multicultural evangelism from this story. First, take note of Jesus' rhythm of intentionality. Jesus placed himself in an environment where he would have social contact with a non-Jewish person. He sat at a well where he knew the chances of interaction with a Samaritan woman were high.

In my life, I have found that if I don't place myself where non-Christians hang out, I can become quite insular as a pastor in my church bubble. It is important for me to play basketball at non-Christian facilities instead of joining Christian basketball leagues if I want to rub shoulders with areligious people. I have discovered that joining the local chamber of commerce or sitting on secular boards in the community expands my opportunities for evangelism. Likewise, if one wants to be in a secular environment where people come from different cultures and backgrounds, one will need to shop and socialize in a different setting. Intentionality is a rhythm of evangelism.

Because I'm married to a woman who is half Korean, our kids classify themselves as tan, or peanut butter, as we like to say around the house. We teach them that God made all flavors and that they are all different but tasty. This helps the young ones understand that difference is just different and not better or worse. We have a lot of "vanilla" and some "chocolate" people in our neighborhood, but we haven't seen a whole lot of "peanut butter" folk. However, there is a large flea market ten minutes from where we live. Whenever I take my kids there they comment on all the "tan" people. The

Latino population comes en masse to the flea market, along with a solid number of Asians. One Saturday morning when I took my sons with me, one of my boys said with a large smile on his face, "Daddy, look at all the peanut-butter people here, just like me." In that moment I realized that even a five-year-old child needs to see others who are his same color to validate his uniqueness.

I now know that we can choose to drive ten minutes in one direction to the drug store to pick up batteries for my son's electronic game or we can drive ten minutes in the opposite direction to the flea market to get the same batteries (less expensive too!). One choice would place us among a lot of vanilla people, with some chocolate. The other would place us among peanut-butter and chocolate people, with some vanilla highlights. Although we're just getting batteries, the choice can make all the difference in the world to my child, who is developing his self-image and view of others.

Additionally, the conversations we have and the connections we make while shopping could lead to a "woman at the well" level conversation. The important thing about this rhythm is to know that the conversation can happen only if we're in the context. Jesus placed himself in the context of the Samaritan woman's world and then the conversation followed.

Jesus' Rhythm of Insight

Another dance lesson we can learn from Jesus is his rhythm of insight. Because he was the Son of God, Jesus knew the history, heritage, and hurt of the woman at the well. But because we are not Jesus, we don't have the insight that Jesus had. Therefore, we must listen and learn. As we listen to the stories of others, we learn their hurts, history, and heritage along the way. The woman at the well identified herself as a Samaritan and a woman. Why? Could it be because society made an issue of her racial- and gender-based inferiority? Is it possible that her race and gender meant something negative to her?

I'm often asked why black people have to make a big deal about being black. Why can't they just ignore their color so that we can all be color-blind? The same question could be asked of this woman. If Jesus didn't bring it up, why would she? If her color, class, and culture didn't matter to Jesus, why would they matter to her?

Could it be that the Samaritan woman's color, class, and culture did matter to Jesus and that is why he was intentional about meeting her? Could it be that Jesus wasn't ignoring the woman's heritage but proactively communicating value to her beyond her social status? I say absolutely! Was Jesus advocating color-blind dancing? I say no! Jesus' rhythm of insight took the woman's culture and class into account as he ministered to her. Notice that he didn't rebuke her for speaking of her gender or accuse her of "playing the race card." Jesus knew that Samaritans were viewed as second-class citizens. He knew women were discriminated against, and that this woman in particular was looked down on because of her sin. Yet in his sovereign love and grace, he reached across those lines to communicate the gospel of salvation as he validated her.

Shouldn't we be as insightful as Jesus? If so, then learning the rhythm of insight through listening to others' history, heritage, and hurt is critical.

Jesus' Rhythm of Identification

Jesus' rhythm of identification is also a lesson worth learning. Jesus identified with the Samaritan woman on a very basic level. He needed water. A social system surrounded the drawing of water—who drew it, who got the best water, whether it was ceremonially unclean to touch the same vessel a non-Jew did. Jesus demonstrated that he needed something that the woman could provide. She had access to something he needed. As soon as they were on common ground, the barriers of race, culture, religion, class, and gender came down and Jesus was able to show the woman that he had something she needed. Wouldn't this be a wonderful rhythm to learn as we practice the dance of multicultural evangelism?

Jesus' Rhythm of Instruction

The final dance lesson we can learn from Jesus is his rhythm of instruction. Notice that when the disciples returned to find Jesus interacting with the woman, Jesus took the time to instruct them on how they should relate to others. Jesus was training his disciples to do multicultural evangelism because he knew that one day these very men would be his witnesses to Jerusalem, Judea, and, that's right, Samaria, and then to the ends of the earth (Acts 1:8). In John 4:35–38 Jesus specifically instructed his disciples to reap the harvest through evangelism. He was teaching them how to work in fields that they were not used to, new fields that he had prepared for harvesting. They had not seen multicultural evangelism like this before, but it was a dance lesson that would prepare them for the rhythms of Pentecost and beyond.

⑥

Ambassadors of reconciliation must learn to dance like Jesus did as he moved and grooved to the rhythms of intentionality, insight, identification, and instruction when building bridges of racial reconciliation. Are you willing to learn new rhythms of evangelism? Is there a different market or grocery store where you can shop that will let you rub shoulders with people of different colors and cultures? Are you willing to listen to and learn from other people in order to gain insight about them and their culture? In so doing, what common ground can you identify? Finally, I ask you, will you instruct others about these lessons in your small group, church, or circle of Christian friends?

When the church begins to groove like Jesus did, it will discover that the power of the Spirit will bring about a sense of unity that allows the entire body to dance. In the next chapter we will learn how this happens.

chapter thirteen

DANCEFORMATION

I WAS SITTING IN MY USUAL SEAT AT CHURCH, THINKING this was going to be a regular Sunday. The auditorium filled with the sounds of praise as the worship team led the congregation in euphoric adoration of Jesus. Everyone was clapping their hands and tapping their feet. Then J. P., a young Korean man with a streak of blond hair, glided onto center stage with Dante, a teenage African-American male with braided hair. They began to dance. The congregation, gripped by the sight of two youths from different, sometimes warring cultures using their creative talents in a unified manner to praise God, broke out in applause.

Many of us had witnessed Dante's rhythmic moves before, but this was J. P.'s debut. He had arrived in the United States only a couple of months before and could not speak a lick of English. While it's not unusual to see the art form of dance incorporated in the worship service at Bridgeway Community Church, the sight of these two dancing together was electrifying. Add the rhythm of the drums, guitars, keyboards, and saxophone and we were having a Jesus party. When J. P. suddenly broke into a rap solo in Korean, echoed by Dante in English . . . whoosh!

This was an unprecedented event even in our church. We witnessed our core value of reconciliation preached more powerfully than any sermon. Two young people from opposite sides of the world came together to worship God, and they could do so because they had the freedom to dance.

Similarly, we as Christians have been likened to a body that must flow and synergize in order to work well. "The body is a unit, though it is made up of many parts; and though all its parts are many, they form one body," says the apostle Paul in 1 Corinthians. "But in fact God has arranged the parts in the body, every one of them, just as he wanted them to be. If they were all one part, where would the body be? As it is, there are many parts, but one body" (12:12, 18–20).

The context of Paul's comments centers on the various spiritual gifts that God has endowed to the church through the Holy Spirit. Have you ever thought about this: Paul doesn't end his conversation about the diversity of spiritual gifts without mentioning a couple of very important components—race and culture. He says, "For we were all baptized by one Spirit into one body—whether Jews or Greeks, slave or free—and we were all given the one Spirit to drink" (v. 13). After this profound statement, Paul exclaims, "Now the body is not made up of one part but of many" (v. 14). I challenge you to read the following section with racial reconciliation in mind:

> The eye cannot say to the hand, "I don't need you!" And the head cannot say to the feet, "I don't need you!" On the contrary, those parts of the body that seem to be weaker are indispensable, and the parts that we think are less honorable we treat with special honor. And the parts that are unpresentable are treated with special modesty, while our presentable parts need no special treatment. But God has combined the members of the body and has given greater honor to the parts that lacked it, so that there should be no division in the body, but that its parts should have equal concern for each other. If one part suffers, every part suffers with it; if one part is honored, every part rejoices with it.
>
> —*1 Corinthians 12:21–26*

When the members of the body of Christ realize that they need each other racially and culturally to express the body's gifts and to serve God and others, they will move beyond the transformation of the mind to the *danceformation* of the body.

I define danceformation as the free-flowing use of spiritual gifts and talents within a multicultural body of believers in an environment where acceptance, freedom, love, and humor prevail in relationships and in the church. The music that gives rhythm to danceformation comes from the Holy Spirit. Paul reminded us that we were all baptized by one Spirit and that as a result, we can dance. God has in his sovereignty elected to give gifts to members of his body regardless of color, class, or culture. We are all equal recipients of God's grace-gifts. Like J. P. and Dante, though we come from different worlds, the music of the Holy Spirit gives us the rhythm to relate, serve, learn, and grow together in synchronized fashion. This is what happened in Acts 2. People from at least fifteen different locations and languages, both Jew and non-Jew, came together and were captivated by a new rhythm of danceformation.

TRANSFORMATION TO DANCEFORMATION

Danceformation must be preceded by transformation. Romans 12:2 says that Christians are to be "transformed by the renewing of their minds" before they are actually ready to know and do the "good, pleasing, and perfect will of God." Then Paul again addresses the topic of unity through the diversity of spiritual gifts just as he did in Corinthians. He says, "Just as each of us has one body with many members, and these members do not all have the same function, so in Christ we who are many form one body, and each member belongs to all the others" (Rom. 12:4–5). On the heels of this emphatic statement, and after listing the various gifts, Paul gives eight practical admonitions in verses 9–13. Transformed minds and transformed members ought to produce the following actions and attitudes:

- Love sincerely (v. 9)
- Hate what is evil; cling to what is good (v. 9b)
- Be devoted to one another above yourselves (v. 10)
- Honor one another above yourselves (v. 10b)
- Keep your zeal and spiritual fervor when serving the Lord (v. 11)

- Be joyful, patient, and faithful in prayer (v. 12)
- Share with God's people who are in need (v. 13)
- Practice hospitality (v. 13b)

These actions and attitudes are not merely self-help maxims we need to aspire to. Rather, if they are going to take root in the life of believers, it will require transformation by the Holy Spirit. The word *transformation* means "metamorphosis or change." Old attitudes about self, others, church, and God must be stripped away and replaced with new motivations, intentions, actions, and attitudes. Only the outpouring of the Holy Spirit can cause people to continually live lives of hospitality, honor, and sincere love.

Danceformation can happen only after those who have been transformed begin to synchronize at a level beyond verbal expression. It's musical. It's rhythmic. It's beyond whether one's church speaks in tongues. It's beyond whether one's ministry is denominational. It's even beyond the style of music or preaching a church may prefer. It's about the free-flowing connection that you and I have because of the unifying power of the Holy Spirit. We are blessed to be brothers and sisters. Because of Christ, we can relate and are related. As the Lord of the dance plays the rhythms of multicultural ministry, whether through psalms, hymns, or spiritual songs, we can move toward danceformation when we are filled with the Holy Spirit.

EVERYDAY LIFE DANCEFORMATION

I conducted a racial reconciliation seminar in the church recently. After several hours of teaching, discussion, lunch, and dialogue, it was time to bring the gathering to a close. I ended the session by reading Jesus' prayer for oneness in John 17. I suggested to the group that since Jesus had to pray for oneness, maybe we should too. Before we could bow our heads, a lady raised her hand to request prayer for her job. As a white nurse in a predominately inner-city black neighborhood, she confessed that she was worn down by dealing with the race issue, especially in her difficult field of work. Trying to show the love of Christ in the city was becoming increasingly burdensome, she tearfully admitted. She requested prayer for energy, strength, and endurance. She also expressed gratefulness for the timeliness of the seminar, as it was renewing her vision for bridge-building.

The moment of beauty came when a Nigerian sister reached across the table and held the hand of the tearful woman and declared that this woman was her personal friend, sister, and a member of her life group. (Life groups are a part of our small-group ministry in the church, in which people gather weekly to "do life" together.) Scooting closer to the nurse were two others from her life group—her Korean fiancé, who placed his arm around her shoulders to comfort her, and another white woman.

Now hold that picture in your mind for a minute. Here is a white woman who is emotionally drained because of the weight of her reconciliation responsibility being surrounded and comforted by a Nigerian woman, a Korean man, and a Caucasian woman. Place that picture in the frame of a racial reconciliation seminar in a multicultural church where John 17 was being taught and prayer requests were being accepted. My friends, this is the kind of snapshot that inspires me to strive toward the vision of what I believe God wants from his church.

What was gratifying to me was that this hurting and tired woman was not in the inner city alone but was being carried by a multicultural life group of praying Christians as she struggled through her daily challenges with race relations. Right in front of me I saw a demonstration of the Holy Spirit working out the practical application of Romans 12. Love, in that moment (and I suspect in that multicultural small group), was indeed sincere.

Would that this picture could be repeated in churches across the land! If we had video cameras running in your church, or in the churches within five miles of yours, what might we see? In no way am I suggesting that Bridgeway is perfect, but in that moment I witnessed a picture-perfect snapshot of the way it ought to be in Christian churches! I long for more pictures like that in my church and in yours.

⟨6⟩

We will discover in the final chapter that, just like the body needs every part, it takes two feet to practice the dance of multicultural ministry. But first we must discard the broken record of the past and listen to the sounds of harmony that God intended.

chapter fourteen

DANCING WITH BOTH FEET

O YOU HAVE MEMORIES OF ATTENDING YOUR HIGH school prom? Dare I tell you one of mine? I remember escorting a girl whom I was googly-eyed over for a while during those years. We first went to dinner at a high-end but intimate restaurant in Washington, D.C., in an area known as Georgetown. In an atmosphere set by freshly cut floral centerpieces, candles, and live background music, we stared at each other romantically, basking in puppy love. We were scheduled to head for the prom after dinner, but guess what? The prom had a reputation of being formal and boring. It was so much more exhilarating, freeing, and fun to be at that restaurant that we never made it to the prom! (Please don't tell my parents!)

CHURCH LUNACY

In Taylor County, Georgia, the prom of 2002 was going to be anything but boring or irrelevant for one high school. It was the talk of the town. Why? It would be the first time in more than thirty years that the prom would be racially integrated. For over three decades this Southern high school had held two proms, one white and one black. The school was approximately half black and half white, and the kids were conditioned to simply go along with the way things had always been. That was until a seventeen-year-old African-American girl by the name of Gerica McClary stepped up along with others in her class to campaign for one prom. That's right, a campaign for one, racially unified school prom! No, friends, this is not the sixties. I am speaking of 2002!

Gerica and others led the campaign throughout the academic year and successfully received the support of students, teachers, and administrators to have one prom. For one school to have separate racial proms was lunacy in the minds of many students. Regardless of the past, common sense screamed, "Lunacy!"

The news about the impending prom hit the national press. One school board official stated that the older folks could learn a lot from the kids on this matter of race. On May 3, 2002, the prom went off without a hitch. Whites, blacks, and others showed up in their limos, gowns, and tuxedos for an evening of high school socialization. A school survey showed that approximately 75 percent of the students were behind the one prom idea.

Isn't it amazing when you look in from the outside how loony some things appear? From the outside, when we look at a racially mixed school having two proms, it seems like lunacy. It's almost unbelievable that no one else noticed or even cared until this seventeen-year-old prophetic voice said, "Hello, has anyone noticed that we are one school attending two proms?"

I wonder if people view the church in like manner. Do people outside our stained-glass windows and beyond the sound of our praise bands view the church as a backward institution stuck in the sixties? I wonder how many people fail to actually make it to church services on Sundays because of their reputation for being boring, or worse, irrelevant to their lives.

As one body, one church, one people, why is it that families who live in the same city awake on Sunday mornings, dress themselves and their children, pile in a car, and drive to their white proms, black proms, Korean proms, and Latino proms? What is that about? That's crazy. That's lunacy. I wonder if there are any Gerica McClary's out there who will speak up and say, "Hello, has anyone noticed that we are one body attending separate proms?"

THE TWO FEET OF EVANGELISTIC WITNESS
Love

Jesus commanded his disciples three times in John 13:34–35 to "love one another." He began by saying, "A new command I give you." What was new about this command? In the Old Testament, loving God and one's neighbor was a foundational command. Yet Jesus stated that this is a new command. Notice that the first time Jesus told the disciples to love one another, it was an exhortation. The second time, it was intensified by his example. Jesus said, "As I have loved you, so you must love one another" (v. 34b). This example of Jesus' love and service made the command new. The disciples, and the Jews who lived prior to the disciples had never seen love personified through the life of Jesus. As Jesus' earthly ministry was coming to an end, he was now instructing his disciples to love as they had seen him love, and more specifically to do so through serving each other in the same way he demonstrated by washing the disciples' feet the evening of the Last Supper. Loving each other through selfless service will clue others in that you are my disciples, Jesus insisted, repeating the command for a third time.

The first time was an exhortation. The second time was to intensify the command by his example. But the third time was to be the evidence to the world that those who love this way are truly followers of Christ. Jesus said, "By this everyone will know that you are my disciples, if you love one another" (v. 35 TNIV).

Let me raise a series of questions: Do you think that the onlooking world sees the church as a place of love? Do you think a watching world sees evidence of love when we attend our racially segregated churches? What if you were seen in your driveway hugging people from a different color or culture before they drove away from your home after a Bible study? What kind of message would it send if your multiracial small group were serving the homeless together, or represented at a community event together? I truly believe that loving one another is critical evidence of our true faith.

Yet love is only one foot of our evangelistic witness. Jesus said, "By this everyone will know that you are my disciples, if you love one another." Honestly, as an evangelist, I am not satisfied with people simply knowing that I'm a disciple of Jesus Christ. Are you? I want non-Christian people to cross the line from unbelief to belief. How does this happen?

Unity

It happens when love is paired with unity. Jesus never meant for love to stand alone as the only foot of our evangelistic witness. If the church is to stand, and even dance, it also needs the foot of unity. Have you noticed Jesus' master prayer in John 17? It is his longest recorded prayer. Out of a myriad of things Jesus could have prayed for in his last days on the earth, he prayed for unity and oneness. Jesus prayed for unity among his disciples and unity among believers in our day. Jesus said, "My prayer is not for them alone," speaking of his disciples, "I pray also for those who will believe in me through their message." That is you, me, and all those believers in generations to come. What was it that Jesus prayed for us? Unity! In John 17:21 he prayed "that all of them may be one, Father, just as you are in me and I am in you. May they also be in us so that the world may believe that you have sent me." Notice the last part again, "so that the world may believe that you have sent me."

By love the world will know that we are Christ's disciples, but by unity the world will believe that Jesus was sent by God. Love and unity are the one-two punch of evangelism. When love and unity move together in your church and mine, it is like dancing with both feet. A lot of churches are hopping on one foot. Yet God is calling us to sincere love and visible unity. In fact, Jesus put an exclamation point on this thought in John 17:23 when he cried out in prayer, "May they be brought to complete unity to let the world know that you sent me and have loved them even as you have loved me!"

Wow! Complete unity, Jesus said. Would this not include racial unity? In fact, when Jesus died on the cross he shattered the greatest barrier that divides humans—the barrier of race and culture.

No wonder the apostle Paul addressed the power of Jesus' death and its power to break down racial walls: "For he himself is our peace, who has made the two one and has destroyed the barrier, the dividing wall of hostility" (Eph. 2:14). One of the purposes of Jesus' death, according to Paul, "was to create in himself one new humanity out of the two, thus making peace, and in this one body to reconcile both of them to God through the cross, by which he put to death their hostility" (Eph. 2:15–16 TNIV). Did you notice the language of "one new humanity" in Ephesians 2 and "complete unity" in John 17? Wouldn't you agree that it is lunacy for those who are a part of one body, as one new humanity under one Lord, to go to two proms?

Will you be that prophet, like Gerica McClary, who stands up to say, "This is lunacy"? Will you become a part of the solution with me and work to have one multicultural prom? Will you accept the mission from God as an ambassador of reconciliation? Will you proclaim the message of reconciliation? Will you accept the ministry of reconciliation? Will you model reconciliation in your relationships?

If you do not act, speak, learn, grow, build new relationships, and cast a vision for multicultural unity to be expressed in your life and ministry, then we are in danger of being here three decades from now with the same old separate proms. The Christian church needs many other visionaries to arise with a voice like Gerica's. Your church needs that voice. Your family needs that voice. Your children need that voice. Will you accept the call to be that voice?

LUNITY

I never made it to my prom because my date and I concluded that it had nothing to offer that was better than our dinner date. We viewed the prom as boring and unworthy of our attention. So we chose not to attend. May this never be the way people view the Christian church from the outside!

The church must dance with both feet to the rhythm of the Holy Spirit. Love and unity together constitute the marriage of John 13 (the great command) and 17 (the great coming together). The bride of Christ must dance with two feet in a world in which people are tripping and falling with no rhythm for life, love, or true unity. But the rhythm for our dance comes from the music of the Holy Spirit, which John addresses in chapters 14–16 of his gospel. The Holy Spirit not only is the link between John 13 and 17 but also is the rhythmic connection between love and unity in the body of Christ. The sounds of lunacy in the church must be replaced with the melodies of "lunity" —the harmony between love and unity. This will cause the watching world to open its ears and heart to a new song of salvation.

My greatest hope is that the church will be a place of lunity, practicing the dance of multicultural ministry with both feet. I pray that this book has informed and inspired you to be a person who moves and grooves in relationships with people from different colors and cultures in life and ministry. I think the alternative is lunacy!

For Gerica McClary the alternative of segregated proms was indeed lunacy. But what's worse is that the vision seemingly died when the visionary moved on. After Gerica and her fellow visionaries graduated, you'll never guess what happened. In May of 2003, one year later, the high school went back to having a white prom and a black prom.

That's unbelievable, isn't it? Sad, actually. Without intentionality, without a vision, without a voice of conscience, people simply revert to what is easy and what is natural. The mantle was dropped because no one else accepted the call.

There are times when I've wearied of finding the unique rhythm for multicultural ministry in my church. Yet every time I stand before my multicultural congregation or receive an e-mail like the one I'm about to share with you, I am inspired to press on, write on, preach on, teach on, train on, run on, and pray on. I've accepted the call. Will you join me?

I'll never go to church with whites

Dear Pastor,

I'm the short black woman that came to you during the Success Symposium and said, "You've changed my life." When you asked me to elaborate, I whispered that in the past I'd thought, "I'd never join a church with white people." I thought of churches as some sort of closed-door meeting place for African-Americans; there we could come and vent over the Rodney King beatings, affirmative action, and the like (that thought is funny to me now). Well let me just say I love going to church with white, yellow, and light brown people. God's people and their cultures make a beautiful rainbow. In the recent past, I along with my prior pastor in the "black church" were Christian racists (what an oxymoron). I'd work with whites and befriend one or two, but the racial stereotypes and animosities ran deeper than I realized. My own past brushes with racists or "racism stories," as you say, surely ignited these feelings. In short, my family and I are very happy at Bridgeway! [I] love the ministries, the Word, the people and the burden of racism that is lifted off my shoulders.

CONCLUSION

Crescendo

THERE ARE CERTAIN PLACES IN A CONCERTO WHERE the sounds of all the instruments resound with great intensity. As the sound builds toward what feels like an anticipated eruption, the height of the sound may suddenly descend to softer moments of calm.

There may be several crescendos throughout a classical piece. So it is with the value of racial reconciliation in the church. So it is in our relationships with God and each other. There are times when we dance freely and effortlessly, but there are also times when the flow is slow. As Christians continue to play from a common sheet of music, the church must crescendo to levels of racial unity and oneness that can be enjoyed, celebrated, and honored by all.

It is okay to appreciate the calmer sounds of racial progress during certain sections of the concerto, but we must always be sure that we are progressing toward the great crescendo of eternity. When we get to heaven, the crescendo of God's glory shared by those in his eternal symphony of the redeemed from every color and culture will never end.

Are you in God's orchestra? The good news of salvation is reflected in the poetic thought below written by an unknown author. The dance of eternal life truly begins with accepting God through placing one's faith in the Lord Jesus Christ. From that point on one can dance with God and others to the rhythms of grace. I hope you dance!

Guidance

When I meditated on the word guidance, I kept seeing "dance" at the end of the word.
I remember reading that doing God's will is a lot like dancing.
When two people try to lead, nothing feels right.
The movement doesn't flow with the music,
and everything is quite uncomfortable and jerky.

When one person lets the other lead, both bodies begin to flow with the music.
One gives gentle cues, perhaps with a nudge to the back or by pressing lightly in one
direction or another. It's as if two become one body, moving beautifully.
The dance takes surrender, willingness, and attentiveness from one person
and gentle guidance and skill from the other.

My eyes drew back to the word guidance. When I saw g, I thought of God,
followed by u and i. God=u=and=i=dance! God, you, and I dance.
This statement is what guidance means to me.

As I lowered my head, I became willing to trust that I would get guidance about my
life. Once again, I became willing to let God lead.

—*Author Unknown*

DAVID'S DO-SOMETHING LIST

Practical Suggestions for Readers
Who Want to Take Action

DONATE YOUR SERVICE TO ANOTHER GROUP OF PEOPLE

Donating your time and effort to serving others not only fulfills you personally but also demonstrates the love of Jesus. Whether you are serving the poor, the aged, widows, orphans, or the imprisoned, regardless of color or culture, you will be extending the compassion of Christ. Is there a mission, a shelter, a clothing consignment store, or a church ministry within an hour's drive where you can volunteer at least once per month? Grab a friend and go for it!

OPEN YOUR HEART

Ask God to help you get a handle on any negative attitude you might have toward a race of people. Prayerfully repent and ask God to root this out of your heart.

Reconciliation begins in the heart, so that is where we must start. Ask God to open your heart to the issues of reconciliation and accept the call to be an ambassador of reconciliation from this point forward, even if you don't fully understand what it will entail.

START BUILDING BRIDGES

Think of three or four settings where you can place yourself to build relationships with people from different racial backgrounds. For example, think about where you live, go to church, shop, buy gas, work out, go to the library, or socialize.

Befriend others who are different from you as the Lord provides opportunities. Be on the lookout for the doors God is opening, and walk through them by faith.

Church leaders can extend invitations to church leaders from other racial backgrounds for ministry opportunities that range from social fellowship between congregants to pulpit swapping and other joint ventures.

OFFER YOUR RESOURCES

What ministries do you support? Are they all white, all black, all Latino, all Asian, or some other unicultural group?

What vendors, manufacturers, and legal services do you contract with? What authors and books do you read? Look at your shelves and identify the color and culture of 90 percent of the authors. What businesses do you support? What missionary efforts do you give to? What banks hold your resources?

More often than not, people tend to support unicultural efforts without thinking about the fact that the organizations they support are not diverse. The leadership, mission, vision, and direction of the agencies, ministries, or companies you are supporting may be racially segregated with no intention to change. Why not consider using your resources to support reconciliation instead of helping organizations that perpetuate segregation?

MEMORIZE THE TRUTH

Jesus said, "Sanctify them by the truth; your word is truth" (John 17:17). God's Word in the hearts of God's people equips us with God's power and authority. Commit to memory the following six Scripture passages and meditate on what they mean.

> 2 Corinthians 5:17–20
> Matthew 28:19–20
> Ephesians 2:14
> John 17:23
> Galatians 3:28
> Acts 17:26

EDUCATE YOURSELF

I truly believe that reading books on race relations and multi-cultural ministry is critical for the process of learning and listening. By reading this book, you have already moved in the right direction. I've also included a book list to help you continue the journey.

Consider taking a college course in cultural diversity, race relations, African-American history, or other sociological areas that may expand your learning. I also suggest that you get the syllabus and suggested reading from these classes whether or not you take the course. The references will be valuable to your library.

TEACH AND TRAIN

If you are a pastor or church leader, begin to think through the core values and mission of your ministry to evaluate its consistency with the ministry of reconciliation. Begin to teach those who are following you about the biblical perspective on race.

This book has many Bible references, outlines, and stories that will give you more than enough material to build on. I don't doubt that you are gifted beyond what is in this book to preach and teach as God grants you special favor. Put the subjects of race, reconciliation, and matters of justice on your preaching or teaching schedule to open the eyes and ears of God's people with "Thus saith the Lord."

Lay people and everyday Christ-followers: train your children and friends with confrontation when you hear or see racism or prejudice. Use these incidents as teachable moments to help redirect people toward God's will for racial unity, equality, and inclusion.

HIRE TOWARD THE VISION

If you are a church leader with authority to hire, why not give extra consideration to someone who reflects the population you desire to reach? This makes sense strategically. My doctoral research showed that multicultural churches had multicultural staffs, while unicultural churches did not. In other words, those who led multicultural churches staffed their leadership team to reflect the diversity they already had or desired to have in their congregation.

To find qualified candidates, one must network within those people groups. Attending multicultural conferences and events, for example, can place you among possible candidates.

INVITE AND INVOLVE THOSE ON THE FRINGES

The power of a personal invitation is incredible. In a church, people will come to an event they might not otherwise attend if someone simply puts an arm around them to extend a warm invitation. Think of someone in your church who may be on the fringes. Think of that person who may be a minority. Invite them to your small group, to your home, to sit with you at a church event, or to some other function. In addition, church leaders should proactively involve those who are underrepresented in the church. By doing this, other underrepresented people from that group will be inspired to increase their service as they recognize that the "coast is clear" for them to succeed.

NETWORK AROUND THE TOPIC OF RECONCILIATION

If you're a pastor, why not pass this book on to another pastor as a gift and schedule a time to discuss it? Or give another book on the subject of race to a church leader and ask for their opinion once they've read it.

If you are looking for a church, this is the time to embrace the value of racial reconciliation and multicultural ministry as you search. If you can't find a multicultural church, find one that has the desire to move in this direction. Interviewing the pastor or designated church leaders will give you a feel for their heart. God may be bringing you to that church as an answer to someone's prayers.

Whatever field you're in, whether secular or Christian, network with others who are interested in reconciliation. Most colleges have minority affairs offices and most companies have human resource components that offer programs and training around the topic. Why not attend a multicultural event that is offered by the college or company?

When diverse groups come together to own a vision and project, the collaborative effort has a greater chance of success and of facilitating relational bonding. Building something together often creates camaraderie and teamwork. When two people, two groups, or two churches work together to solve a problem or build a project, the potential of breaking down racial walls is huge.

I chose to join a local board in my community. Other board members eventually got comfortable with having a preacher on their board. Whatever preconceived notion some may have had about preachers was revised because they recognized that I was normal (sort of) like them. What effort in your community can you join that will stretch you in the areas of reconciliation for the purpose of networking and multicultural evangelism?

G ET HELP FROM OTHERS

Consultants can assist your organization in crafting a multiculturally effective ministry for today and the future.

Aside from my organization, the BridgeLeader Network, I know that noted author George Yancy also is active in this area. For information go to www.racialreconciliation.com.

Choose one seminar, workshop, or class to attend this year that promotes reconciliation and diversity to gain more knowledge and understanding. Feel free to check my website at www.BridgeLeader.com to see what conferences and events I will be speaking at or hosting, or link to other ministries from my site for something that may be closer to you.

appendix one

RACIAL RECONCILIATION SURVEY

Thank you for taking time to complete this formal research survey. Please choose one answer for each question and circle the number corresponding to your answer. There are no right or wrong answers, and your responses are completely confidential.

SOCIO-DEMOGRAPHIC INFORMATION

1. My gender is:
   Male. 01
   Female 02

2. My age is . . . . _____ Years

3. My highest grade or year of school completed is:
   Elementary/lower 01 02 03 04 05
   Junior high/middle. 06 07 08
   High school/GED 09 10 11 12
   Associate's degree 13
   Bachelor's degree 14
   Master's degree 15
   Doctoral degree 16

4. My total household income last year was:
   Less than $9,999 01
   $10,000–$14,999 02
   $15,000–$19,999 03
   $20,000–$24,999 04

$25,000–$29,999 05
$30,000–$34,999 06
$35,000–$39,999 07
$40,000–$44,999 08
$45,000–$49,999 09
$50,000–$54,999 10
$55,000–$59,999 11
$60,000–$64,999 12
$65,000 or greater 13

5. My marital status is:
Married 01
Single 02
Separated 03
Divorced 04
Widowed 05

6. My ethnic/cultural background is:
African-American (black) 01
Caucasian (white) 02
Caucasian (Jewish) 03
Oriental/Asian-American 04
Hispanic/Latino 05
Native American 06
Other (please specify): _____ 07

GENERAL FACTUAL INFORMATION

7. Have you made a decision to follow Jesus Christ as your
Lord and Savior?
Yes 01
No 02

8. At approximately what age did you make this decision?
    . . . . _____ Years

9. How long have you been regularly attending Bridgeway
    Community Church? . . . . _____ Years

10. Do you feel like you have ever been discriminated
    against because of your race?
    Yes 01
    No 02

11. Do you have a personal (not professional) friend from
    another race?
    Yes 01
    No 02

12. Have you shared personal time with someone outside of
    your race within the last 60 days? (Dinner, had them in
    your home, shopping, etc.)
    Yes 01
    No 02

13. Do you harbor ill feelings, negative opinions, or
    resentment toward any racial group?
    Yes 01
    No 02
    (if no, skip to question 15)

    a. Toward which group(s) do you harbor these
        negative feelings? (circle one or more)
        African-American (black) 01
        Caucasian (white) 02
        Caucasian (Jewish) 03
        Oriental/Asian-American 04

Hispanic/Latino 05
Native American. 06
Other (please specify): _____ . . . 07

b. What is the primary source of these negative feelings
    or views? (circle only one)
    An unpleasant personal incident. 01
    Family upbringing and beliefs 02
    Unfair society 03
    Sour relationship or friendship 04
    Other (please specify): _____ . . . 05

c. Have your negative feelings changed?
    Yes *(if yes, skip to question 14)* 01
    No 02

d. What experiences would most likely change these
    feelings? (circle up to three)
    A pleasant personal incident. 01
    A more equal society 02
    A positive personal relationship or friendship with
    someone of that race. 03
    A personal (or stronger) relationship with Christ . 04
    Continued involvement at Bridgeway. 05
    Participation in activities that promote
    reconciliation 06
    All of the above 07
    Other (please specify): _____ . . . 08
    (please skip to question 15)

14. What has helped you the *most* to change these feelings?
    (circle only one)

Meaningful dialogue about race 01
A pleasant personal incident 02
Family upbringing and beliefs 03
A more equal society 04
A positive personal relationship or friendship with
someone of that race 05
My personal relationship with Christ 06
Attending Bridgeway Community Church 07
Other (please specify): _____ 08

ATTITUDES AND OPINIONS ABOUT RACE

	strongly disagree	disagree	agree	strongly agree
15. Racial tensions exist within Bridgeway Community Church 1		2	3	4
16. Racial tensions are getting better within American society 1		2	3	4
17. Racial understanding and reconciliation will not improve significantly through dialogue 1		2	3	4
18. The best way for people to develop racial understanding and reconciliation is through multicultural events and/or training 1		2	3	4
19. Racial understanding and reconciliation will not improve by simply living a committed Christian life 1		2	3	4

20. The best way for people to develop racial understanding and reconciliation is through practical Bible teaching on the subject. 1   2   3   4

21. Developing a personal relationship with someone of another race will not significantly improve racial understanding and reconciliation. . . . .
. . . . 1   2   3   4

22. Interracial marriages should not be acceptable in American society. . . 1   2   3   4

23. I would support the interracial marriage of my children.
. . . . 1   2   3   4

24. I feel Bridgeway Community Church is addressing race relations effectively. 1   2   3   4

25. Bridgeway Community Church spends too much time on racial issues. 1   2   3   4

⟲

Thank you for taking the time to complete this research instrument.

appendix two

SIX-SESSION RACIAL RECONCILIATION CURRICULUM

OUTLINE

1.0 The Characteristics of Racism
    1.1   Definition of Racism
    1.2   Six Components of Racism
    1.3   Three Categories of Racism

2.0 The Continuum of Racial Reconciliation
    2.1   Personal Experiences and Upbringing
    2.2   Placement of Self on Continuum

3.0 The Consequences of Racism
    3.1   Causes of Racism
    3.2   The Divine-Human Timeline

4.0 The Calling of a Reconciler
    4.1   Inspiration (vision)
    4.2   Intentionality (mission)
    4.3   Implementation (strategy)
    4.4   Four Truths about the Race Issue

5.0 The Clothing of a Reconciler
    5.1   Old Clothes and New Clothes
    5.2   Three Components (relational, dialogue, educational)

6.0 The Commitment of a Reconciler
    6.1   Study Key Points about Race Relations
    6.2   Review Learning
    6.3   Collect Learning Logs and Any Other Homework
    6.4   Commitment through Prayer to Be a Reconciler

SESSION 1
THE CHARACTERISTICS OF RACISM

1.1   Definition of Racism

1.2   Six Components of Racism

1.3   Three Categories of Racism

LARGE GROUP DISCUSSION
Choose the answer that best represents your motivation.

1.   What motivated you to sign up for this group?
     a.   High interest due to personal feelings
     b.   High interest in learning
     c.   Other: _____

2.   What expectations do you have?
     a.   To share experiences, air opinions, and to contribute
     b.   To absorb information, ask questions, and to
          contemplate
     c.   Other: _____

3.   This group would exceed my expectations if:
     a.   I gained knowledge or learned something that
          assisted me in the process of reconciliation
     b.   I gained an appreciation, awareness, or a better
          understanding of the other race
     c.   Other: _____

SMALL GROUP DISCUSSION
The following two questions will be discussed in groups separated
by white and black and answers will be documented.

1. What is your perception of how it feels to grow up black or white? (answer for the opposite of your race)
2. What things do blacks or whites value? (answer for the opposite of your race)

LARGE GROUP TEACHING TIME

DA's Definition

Racism is when one speaks, acts, or thinks *negatively* about someone because of their color, class, or culture.

Six Components of Racism

1. Reason
2. Attitude/action (such as discrimination)
3. Color, class, culture, or control
4. Ignorance (for example, the "My Brother" adage: "When he saw me from afar, he thought I was a monster and was very scared. When I got a little closer, he thought I was an animal and was just very nervous. But when we stood face to face, he relaxed and breathed with a sigh of relief because he realized that I was his brother.")
5. Stereotype
6. Mentality/motivation of superiority

Three Categories of Racism

1. *Individual:* This is the personal view one holds; it affects people on an individual level.
2. *Institutional:* This is a systemic and sociological condition that creates an environment whereby particular kinds of people are excluded from the positive norms of that institution.

3. *Indirect:* This could be individual, institutional, or the integration of both. However, indirect racism is not a targeted form of racism. It is better described as "neglecting" certain kinds of people from the positive norms of an institution or society as opposed to "creating" such an environment (e.g., A traditional church being unintentionally hostile toward seekers).

CONCLUSION FROM SCRIPTURE

Galatians 3:28
Colossians 3:11
1 Peter 1:22

HOMEWORK

Please write one paragraph to answer each question and bring next week.

1. What is your first memory of someone from the opposite race?
2. What did you learn when you were growing up about the other race from your parents? Church? Television? Movies?

SESSION 2
THE CONTINUUM OF RACIAL RECONCILIATION

2.1   Personal Experiences and Upbringing

2.2   Placement of Self on Continuum

REVIEW
1.   Six components of racism
2.   Three categories of racism

SMALL GROUP DISCUSSION
Two questions were given as homework:

1.   What is your first memory of someone from the opposite race?
2.   What did you learn when you were growing up about the other race from your parents? Church? Television? Movies?

You were supposed to write a one-paragraph answer for each question. Share your paragraph with the small group you are in. When the larger group reunites, tell us what you as an individual, or what your group as a whole, observed or learned from the sharing of your paragraphs.

NEIGHBOR NUDGE
Place yourself on the Racial Reconciliation Continuum. Are you a racist? Are you a reconciler? Or are you somewhere in between?

This continuum parallels to the continuum of faith in evangelism. In evangelism you can assess people's readiness to hear the gospel by identifying them as atheist, cynic, agnostic, or seeker. After a person has converted, he or she is identified as a new believer, also known as a babe in Christ. As the Christian babe grows, he or she becomes a young child, a teen, an adult, and then a mature believer. Below is the continuum with definitions for each term. Identify where you are on the continuum and place an "X" on that spot.

RACIAL RECONCILIATION CONTINUUM

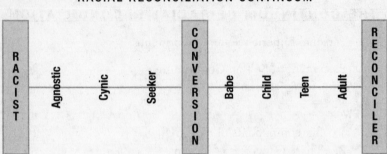

The far left (racist): A racist harbors ill feelings, and possibly hatred, toward a particular person or group of people because of color, class, or culture. Such feelings cause that person to speak, act, or think negatively toward or about this group.

The middle (conversion): In the middle of the continuum is the point or period of "racial reconciliation conversion," as I like to call it. This is the point at which a person realizes that God wants her to deal with issues of race in her own heart or in society. She has awakened to the knowledge that things are desperately wrong. She realizes that God desires her to make a difference first personally and then in society.

Cynics, agnostics, and seekers: Between the racist and the point of conversion are agnostics, cynics, and seekers. An *agnostic* doesn't really care about other races or racial issues and is happy being with his own kind. A *cynic* is pessimistic about real change truly happening and is unwilling to seek out change or make concerted efforts. A *seeker* is somewhat ignorant about other races or racial issues but is willing to learn and has a desire to grow in this new area.

The far right (reconciler): A reconciler is a change agent who understands that God has called him to be an ambassador of reconciliation. This person seeks to develop cross-cultural relationships with those of another race and to be a channel of God's love, grace, justice, and forgiveness through friendships and societal contributions.

Babe, child, teen, and adult: A person who has reached the point of conversion and is ready to move along the continuum will go through four stages of growth: babe, child, teen, adult. A *babe* is newly born in her awareness of racial issues and has come to realize that she needs to deal with issues of race relations if she is going to be all that God has called us to be as reconcilers. She depends on others to help feed her and lead her in the new area of racial reconciliation. A *child* is a young and growing learner who is active in ascertaining knowledge regarding race while trying to apply new knowledge. A child is energetic and excited but lacks discernment when applying the new knowledge in everyday relationships. A *teen* is developing and maturing in the area of reconciliation. The teen is steadily building bridges of reconciliation while periodically failing in doing so. He is winning at times and losing at times as he struggles through the issues and relationships of reconciliation. An *adult* is active in taking responsibility as a reconciler and contributes where she can to make reconciliation happen. The adult is more than a bridge-builder who is still growing and learning; she has become a bridge-leader in that she is far enough ahead to help others to convert and grow. She is a dedicated reproducer.

HOMEWORK
1. Read the article *Perspective* by David Anderson.
2. Make entries into your Learning Log.
3. Write down in one paragraph what you think it will take for you to grow from where you are on the continuum to the next progress point. Turn this into me next week.

CONCLUSION FROM SCRIPTURE
2 Corinthians 5:16–21 (The mission, ministry, and message of reconciliation)

SESSION 3
THE CONSEQUENCES OF RACISM

3.1   Causes of Racism

3.2   The Divine-Human Timeline

REVIEW

1. Six components of racism
2. Three categories of racism
3. 2 Corinthians 5 teaches that Christians have been given two things regarding reconciliation. What are they?

NEIGHBOR NUDGE

Share your paragraph from last week's homework assignment with your neighbor. You were supposed to write "What you think it will take for you to grow from where you are on the continuum to the next progress point." Turn this into me tonight.

LARGE GROUP EXERCISE

Name out loud, as I write on the board, every racial problem, issue, or incident you can think of. *(These are the consequences of racism.)*

LARGE GROUP BIBLE STUDY

We will look at the following passages together as a large group and discover God's overall perspective regarding racism and mankind in general:

Genesis 1–2
Genesis 3:1–16
Genesis 4:1–12
Genesis 6:5–14
Genesis 6:18
Genesis 9:9

Genesis 9:18–10:20
Genesis 11:1–9
Genesis 12:1–3
Genesis 15
Exodus 1
Exodus 3:1–17
all four Gospels
Acts 2:1–21
Acts 2:41–47
Galatians 3:26–29

FINAL QUESTION

As a result of this study what observations can we make regarding racism in America? The world?

BOTTOM LINE

Racism and its consequences are a product of *sin*, not *skin!* As God's chosen people we are called to live a life of righteousness that demonstrates love, forgiveness, and acceptance.

SESSION 4
<u>THE CALLING OF A RECONCILER</u>

4.1   Inspiration (vision: what I am inspired to become.)

4.2   Intentionality (mission: what I will intentionally do.)

4.3   Implementation (strategy: how I will do it.)

4.4   Four Truths about the Race Issue

REVIEW

1.   Six components of racism
2.   Three categories of racism
3.   The cause of racism is what? And not what?
4.   What is "Divine Segregation"? Where can it be found in Scripture?
5.   When was "Divine Integration"? Where can it be found in Scripture?
6.   What common language do the people of God speak?

SMALL GROUP DISCUSSION

As Christians, our *Inspiration* (vision) comes from the word of God and the Holy Spirit working in our lives.

1.   Read and reread this Scripture passage about reconciliation: 2 Corinthians 5:16–21. This passage teaches that Christians have been given two things regarding reconciliation. The *ministry* and the *message* of reconciliation.

2.   Discussion Questions
     a.   Discuss your understanding of God's vision for reconciliation.

    b.   How does this inspire you personally?

    c.   What is your personal vision for reconciliation?

LARGE GROUP LESSON

This lesson is designed to help facilitate the *Implementation* Process: Handout titled *Four Truths about the Race Issue.*

HOMEWORK

As Christians, it is important to proactively and *Intentionally* commit to doing something (mission), lest we fall into passive patterns reflecting little change. Once we intend to do something that we have been inspired to do, it is still not easy to follow through. Therefore, the homework below is designed to help you think through the *Implementation* (strategy) of what you are committed to doing and becoming. *Prayerfully think through and write out the answers to these questions:*

1. What is God saying to you about this issue of reconciliation as it personally relates to you?

2. Once this group ends, what will you commit to doing to intentionally become a reconciler? How and when will you do it?

FOUR TRUTHS ABOUT THE RACE ISSUE

1. *Reconciliation is a theological issue:* In order to be a reconciler you must have a theological head (mind).

    a.   An application of the Great Commission and Great Commandment (Matt. 28:18–20; John 17:23; cf., John 13:35).

    b.   Acceptance of others within the body is biblically grounded (Rom. 15:1–7).

    c.   Ambassador of reconciliation is every believers calling (2 Cor. 5:17–20).

      d. Attachment to one another as siblings is a truth
that must be grasped (Rom. 12:4–5).

2. *Reconciliation is a personal issue:* In order to be a
reconciler you must have a broken heart.
    a. Old clothes must come off (Col. 3:5–8).
    b. Forgiveness must take place (Col. 3:13).

3. *Reconciliation is a relational issue:* In order to be a
reconciler you must exercise healing hands.
    a. New clothes must be on (Col. 3:12).
    b. Unity must be maintained (Eph. 4:3).
    c. Reconciliation takes initiative (Matt. 5:23–24).

4. *Reconciliation is a social issue:* In order to be a reconciler
you must understand social history and hysteria.
    a. The world has a sociological viewpoint that must
be understood but not "bought into" (1 John 4:1–6;
5:19–21).
    b. Whites who learn the social history of blacks
demonstrate care, concern, and a unique understanding that will allow them to build bridges in
a loving way.
    c. Minorities who learn their own history may find a
sense of gratefulness (ethnic pride) which may help
them to feel better about themselves and their
ancestors.

Warning: be careful not to allow Satan to turn your knowledge
into a weapon of anger and hate.

PRACTICAL APPLICATION

How can I help the process of race relations in my personal life, my family, my church, and my world?

1. *Representation:* If point 1 is correct (that reconciliation is a theological issue), then reconciliation must be modeled and taught to others through me as an ambassador.

2. *Repentance:* If point 2 is correct (that reconciliation is a personal issue), then I must confess my sins of racism, prejudice, favoritism, ignorance, apathy, and anger, before my God (and possibly my brothers and sisters) and turn away from such behavior.

3. *Relationships:* If point 3 is correct (that reconciliation is a relational issue), then I must live and model reconciling relationships with others before my Lord and before other people to demonstrate the love of Christ through human contact.

4. *Role:* If point 4 is correct (that reconciliation is also a social issue), then I must consider what role God wants me to play in the sociopolitical culture that may effect social change.

SESSION 5
THE CLOTHING OF A RECONCILER

5.1   Old Clothes and New Clothes

5.2   Three Components (relational, dialogue, educational)

REVIEW

1. Six components of racism
2. Three categories of racism
3. The cause of racism is what? And not what?
4. What is "Divine Segregation"? Where can it be found
    in Scripture?
5. When was "Divine Integration"? Where can it be found
    in Scripture?
6. What common language do the people of God speak?
7. What "reconciliation" Scripture passage calls all
    Christians to be reconcilers?
8. This passage tells us that we have been given two
    things. What are they?
9. There are four truths about the race issue. For example
    "Reconciliation is a *social* issue."
10. What other kind of issue is reconciliation?

SMALL GROUP REVIEW

Break into three groups. Discuss the answers to the above review
questions without using your notes. Once you have completed the
group review of all the questions, then you may go to your notes to
find, verify, and clarify your answers.

LARGE GROUP EXERCISE
Discussion

If you were asked how you would help solve the race relations con-
flicts in a church or Christian organization, or some secular organi-

zation, how would you go about it? (Fact: Maybe you've heard that we learn 10 percent of what we read, 20 percent of what we hear, 30 percent of what we see, 50 percent of what we both see and hear, 70 percent of what we discuss with others, 80 percent of what we experience personally, and 95 percent of what we teach someone else.

Three Essential Elements When Teaching Others about Reconciliation

1. *Relational Element:* Apply the "new clothes" characteristics and discover where that person, group, or organization needs to grow.

2. *Dialogue Element:* Communication and language are gifts from God. It is often true that through dialogue and discussion greater understanding is achieved. Remember the adage: "When he saw me from afar, he thought I was a monster and was very scared. When I got a little closer, he thought I was an animal and was just very nervous. But when we stood face to face, he relaxed and breathed with a sigh of relief because he realized that I was his brother." Dialogue and communication bring people even closer together and build relationships.

3. *Education Element:* Ignorance is a major component of racism that needs to be addressed. When people dialogue, they learn of their own misconceptions, stereotypes, and areas of personal and relational growth. Through education people can learn the important values of those who are different. In addition, they will come to appreciate their diversity and celebrate their unity. What are some ways you can become educated about others?

HOMEWORK
1. Turn in a copy of your Learning Log next week.
2. Read the *Alternative View* by Dr. Anthony Evans.

SESSION 6
<u>THE COMMITMENT OF A RECONCILER</u>

6.1   Study Key Points about Race Relations

6.2   Review Learning

6.3   Collect Learning Logs and Any Other Homework

6.4   Commit through Prayer to Be a Reconciler

LARGE GROUP DISCUSSION

1.   Read John 17 together to visit the idea of unity, oneness or "communion."
2.   Explain the following sentence: "Coping begins with comprehending."
3.   How important do you think comprehending is to the reconciliation process?
4.   What do you think it takes to comprehend what others are feeling?
5.   Are Christians called to do more than cope with racial tension within the church? Explain.

PRACTICAL EXERCISE

Remember where you placed yourself on the Racial Reconciliation Continuum?

RACIAL RECONCILIATION CONTINUUM

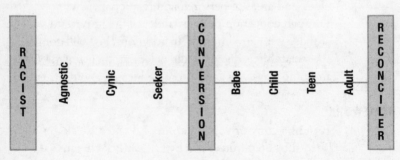

Now match your position with the Continuum of Reconciliation.

THE CONTINUUM OF RECONCILIATION

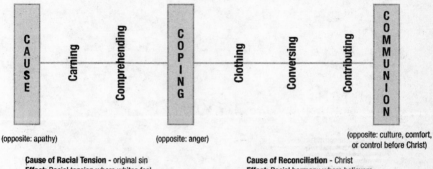

(opposite: apathy) (opposite: anger) (opposite: culture, comfort, or control before Christ)

Cause of Racial Tension - original sin
Effect: Racial tension where whites feel guilty, angry, defensive, and blacks feel angry, resentful, and justified.

Cause of Reconciliation - Christ
Effect: Racial harmony where believers commune as one with God and each other.

If you identified yourself as a *racist, cynic, agnostic,* or *seeker,* you need to focus on Caring, Comprehending, or Coping.

If you identified yourself as a *babe* you should focus on Clothing.

If you identified yourself as a *child* or *teen,* you need to focus on Conversing.

If you identified yourself as an *adult* or *reconciler,* you should focus on Contributing.

Everyone should try to contribute in some way. Although many areas will overlap, having a specific area of focus and growth can help you move from one step to the next. What is your plan or commitment to be a contributor toward communion (reconciliation)?

CLOSING SCRIPTURE

Ephesians 2:11–22; 4:3

RECOMMENDED READING

While I don't endorse all the positions these books take, I can recommend them because of the variety of opinions they hold. Review of the material will give the reader an awareness of the variety of viewpoints and opinions held on the volatile issue of race.

☙

Anderson, David, and Brent Zuercher. *Letters across the Divide*. Grand Rapids: Baker, 2001.

Breckenridge, James and Lillian Breckenridge. *What Color Is Your God?* Wheaton, Ill.: Victor Books, 1995.

Campbell, Bebe Moore. "Coming Together: Can We See beyond the Color of Our Skin?" *Essence* 25, no. 10 (1995): 80.

Cooper, Rodney. *We Stand Together*. Chicago: Moody Press, 1995.

DeYoung, Curtiss Paul, Michael Emerson, George Yancey, and Karen Chai Kim. *United by Faith: The Multiracial Congregation as an Answer to the Problem of Race*. New York: Oxford University Press, 2003.

Emerson, Michael, and Christian Smith. *Divided by Faith: Evangelical Religion and the Problem of Race in America*. New York: Oxford University Press, 2000.

Evans, Anthony. *Let's Get to Know Each Other*. Nashville: Thomas Nelson, 1995.

Hacker, Andrew. *Two Nations*. Wheaton, Ill.: Scripture Press, 1992.

Ham, Ken, Carl Wieland, and Don Batten. *One Blood: The Biblical Answer to Racism*. Green Forest, Ark.: Masters Books, 1999.

Mathias, Barbara, and May Ann French. *Forty Ways to Raise a Nonracist Child*. New York: Harper, 1996.

Perkins, John, and Thomas A. Tarrants III. *He's My Brother.* Grand Rapids: Chosen Books, 1994.

Perkins, Spencer and Chris Rice. *More Than Equals.* Downers Grove, Ill.: InterVarsity Press, 1993.

Reddy, Maureen T., ed. *Everyday Acts against Racism: Raising Children in a Multicultural World.* New York: Avalon Publishing, 1996.

Schaeffer, Francis A. *The Church at the End of the Twentieth Century: The Threat of Silence.* (cf. chap. 6). Downers Grove, Ill.: InterVarsity Press, 1970.

Thernston, Stephan, and Abigail Thernston. *America in Black and White.* New York: Simon and Schuster, 1997.

Washington, Raleigh, and Glen Kehrein. *Breaking Down Walls.* Chicago: Moody Press, 1993.

West, Cornel. *Race Matters.* Boston: Random House, 1994.

Yancey, George A. and Sherelyn Whittum. *Just Don't Marry One.* Valley Forge, Pa.: Judson Press, 2002.

INDEX

WILLOW
Willow Creek Association

Willow Creek Association
Vision, Training, Resources for Prevailing Churches

This resource was created to serve you and to help you in building a local church that prevails!

Since 1992, the Willow Creek Association (WCA) has been linking like-minded, action-oriented churches with each other and with strategic vision, training, and resources. Now a worldwide network of over 6,400 churches from more than ninety denominations, the WCA works to equip Member Churches and others with the tools needed to build prevailing churches. Our desire is to inspire, equip, and encourage Christian leaders to build biblically functioning churches that reach increasing numbers of unchurched people, not just with innovations from Willow Creek Community Church in South Barrington, Illinois, but from any church in the world that has experienced God-given breakthroughs.

WILLOW CREEK CONFERENCES

Each year, thousands of local church leaders, staff and volunteers—from WCA Member Churches and others—attend one of our conferences or training events. Conferences offered on the Willow Creek campus in South Barrington, Illinois, include:

Prevailing Church Conference: Foundational training for staff and volunteers working to build a prevailing local church.

Prevailing Church Workshops: More than fifty strategic, day-long workshops covering seven topic areas that represent key characteristics of a prevailing church; offered twice each year.

Promiseland Conference: Children's ministries; infant through fifth grade.

Student Ministries Conference: Junior and senior high ministries.

Willow Creek Arts Conference: Vision and training for Christian artists using their gifts in the ministries of local churches.

Leadership Summit: Envisioning and equipping Christians with leadership gifts and responsibilities; broadcast live via satellite to eighteen cities across North America.

Contagious Evangelism Conference: Encouragement and training for churches and church leaders who want to be strategic in reaching lost people for Christ.

Small Groups Conference: Exploring how developing a church *of* small groups can play a vital role in developing authentic Christian community that leads to spiritual transformation.

To find out more about WCA conferences, visit our website at www.willowcreek.com.

PREVAILING CHURCH REGIONAL WORKSHOPS

Each year the WCA team leads several, two-day training events in select cities across the United States. Some twenty day-long workshops are offered in topic areas including leadership, next-generation ministries, small groups, arts and worship, evangelism, spiritual gifts, financial stewardship, and spiritual formation. These events make quality training more accessible and affordable to larger groups of staff and volunteers.

To find out more about Prevailing Church Regional Workshops, visit our website at www.willowcreek.com.

WILLOW CREEK RESOURCES™

Churches can look to Willow Creek Resources™ for a trusted channel of ministry tools in areas of leadership, evangelism, spiritual gifts, small groups, drama, contemporary music, financial stewardship, spiritual transformation, and more. For ordering information, call (800) 570-9812 or visit our website at www.willowcreek.com.

WCA MEMBERSHIP

Membership in the Willow Creek Association as well as attendance at WCA Conferences is for churches, ministries, and leaders who hold to a historic, orthodox understanding of biblical Christianity. The annual church membership fee of $249 provides substantial discounts for your entire team on all conferences and Willow Creek Resources, networking opportunities with other outreach-oriented churches, a bimonthly newsletter, a subscription to the *Defining Moments* monthly audio journal for leaders, and more.

To find out more about WCA membership, visit our website at www.willowcreek.com.

WILLOWNET (WWW.WILLOWCREEK.COM)

This Internet resource service provides access to hundreds of Willow Creek messages, drama scripts, songs, videos, and multimedia ideas. The system allows you to sort through these elements and download them for a fee.

Our website also provides detailed information on the Willow Creek Association, Willow Creek Community Church, WCA membership, conferences, training events, resources, and more.

WILLOWCHARTS.COM (WWW.WILLOWCHARTS.COM)

Designed for local church worship leaders and musicians, WillowCharts.com provides online access to hundreds of music charts and chart components, including choir, orchestral, and horn sections, as well as rehearsal tracks and video streaming of Willow Creek Community Church performances.

THE NET (HTTP://STUDENTMINISTRY.WILLOWCREEK.COM)

The NET is an online training and resource center designed by and for student ministry leaders. It provides an inside look at the structure, vision, and mission of prevailing student ministries from around the world. The NET gives leaders access to complete programming elements, including message outlines, dramas, small group questions, and more. An indispensable resource and networking tool for prevailing student ministry leaders!

CONTACT THE WILLOW CREEK ASSOCIATION

If you have comments or questions, or would like to find out more about WCA events or resources, please contact us:

Willow Creek Association
P.O. Box 3188, Barrington, IL 60011-3188
Phone: (800) 570-9812 or (847) 765-0070
Fax: (888) 922-0035 or (847) 765-5046
Web: www.willowcreek.com